Confessions

of 5 Christian Wives

Shauna Mayer

and Hollywood friends

WESTBOW®
PRESS
A DIVISION OF THOMAS NELSON
& ZONDERVAN

Scripture taken from the New King James Version. Copyright 1979, 1980,
1982 by Thomas Nelson, inc. Used by permission. All rights reserved.

Scripture taken from the Contemporary English Version © 1991,
1992, 1995 by American Bible Society, Used by Permission.

Scriptures taken from the Holy Bible, New International Version®, NIV®.
Copyright © 1973, 1978, 1984, 2011 by Biblica, Inc.™ Used by permission of
Zondervan. All rights reserved worldwide. www.zondervan.com The "NIV"
and "New International Version" are trademarks registered in the United
States Patent and Trademark Office by Biblica, Inc.™ All rights reserved.

WestBow Press books may be ordered through booksellers or by contacting:
WestBow Press
A Division of Thomas Nelson & Zondervan
1663 Liberty Drive
Bloomington, IN 47403
www.westbowpress.com
1 (866) 928-1240

Because of the dynamic nature of the Internet, any web addresses or
links contained in this book may have changed since publication and
may no longer be valid. The views expressed in this work are solely those
of the author and do not necessarily reflect the views of the publisher,
and the publisher hereby disclaims any responsibility for them.

Any people depicted in stock imagery provided by Thinkstock are models,
and such images are being used for illustrative purposes only.
Certain stock imagery © Thinkstock.

ISBN: 978-1-4908-2193-1 (sc)
ISBN: 978-1-4908-2192-4 (hc)
ISBN: 978-1-4908-2194-8 (e)

Library of Congress Control Number: 2014900656

Printed in the United States of America.

WestBow Press rev. date: 3/20/2014

"The fact that I am a woman does not make me a different kind of Christian, but the fact that I am a Christian does make me a different kind of woman."

Elisabeth Elliot

Contents

Shauna Mayer
Page 15

Trish Steele
Page 81

Deborah Parker
Page 119

Barbara Allen
Page 153

Proverbs 31: The "Virtuous Wife"
The Beloved Bride of Christ
– by Shauna Mayer
Page 183

Foreword
by Dr. Mary Katherine Baxter

Dr. Mary Katherine Baxter

S hauna Mayer is my dear friend and beloved spiritual daughter of the last seventeen years. We have traveled together and ministered many, many times throughout those years. She is a humble handmaiden and a true servant of God. Shauna is the Proverbs 31 Woman personified, in my opinion.

I have personally witnessed the hardships and tribulations you will read about in her story. I have stood back and marveled at the seemingly endless attacks that she overcame and took in stride as she trusted in God to carry her through. She loves the Lord with all her heart. Her life is a witness of that love and commitment to Him.

She has been talking about this book for the last ten years, which the Lord imparted through a prophetic dream. I am thrilled for her that its time has finally come. God's fingerprints are all over it and His Spirit within it. Her heart is to save and minister to the unsaved, the heartbroken, and the backslidden so they, too, will come to know our loving Lord and Messiah, Jesus Christ, as their personal Savior.

This true story of Shauna's life is unexaggerated and is written with unbelievable candor and transparency for the sole purpose of saving others and to witness the greatness and goodness of our God. Jesus is real! Jesus is alive!

I pray you will be blessed and changed into His image as you read these glorious stories of these godly women as they went from strength to strength, faith to faith, and glory to glory. God will do that for you, too! You've got his Word on it.

Dr. Mary Katherine Baxter, international preacher, evangelist, and best-selling author of *The Divine Revelation of Heaven, The Divine Revelation of Hell,* and seven other *Divine Revelation* books.

Dedication

To the life and memory of Chip Mayer, my former husband and the father of our two daughters. He was alive when I had the vivid prophetic dream of this book. The Lord showed me the beautiful color cover, title, and contents. The following morning I awoke and shared the dream with Chip. I asked if he would object to the writing of the book God had shown me. With no hesitation whatsoever, he admitted he'd been deceived and hamstrung by the Devil and wholeheartedly agreed I should write the book and expose the works of darkness. He went on to say, "I know you will share what I put you through with great grace." That is exactly what I have attempted to do. May God be glorified!

George Charles Mayer III
"Chip"
2/21/1954-7/24/2011

Special Thanks

Olivia Marie Truhlar

Does God still speak to people in dreams? Yes, you better believe He does. That was the genesis of this book. I can take no credit for it. This was entirely God's idea. While sleeping one night more than ten years ago, He showed me this color cover, zoomed in on the title, and downloaded the contents of the book in a vivid dream. I would have never imagined it would take this long to publish. I feel like I've been pregnant for ten long years. But God always has a "due date," or what He calls an "appointed time."

The Lord had someone so loving, caring, and compassionate in mind to be the one to help me birth this. She loves the Lord with all of her heart and cares for others with a depth I've rarely seen in another human being. She believed in me and the idea of this book bringing glory to God and ministering to hurting women.

That special, godly lady is my beloved sister and friend, Olivia Marie Truhlar. I am eternally grateful to God for her and her friendship. Olivia's faith in God and investment in me, with this book, has been life changing. I could not have done this without her, and that's exactly the way God had it planned.

Olivia helped to make my dream come true. Great is your reward. Thank you with all of my heart. I love you dearly.

Shauna's Introduction

Vessel of Mercy, Pearl of Great Price, Living Lampstand

*I*f you've been walking with the Lord Jesus Christ very long and "have ears to hear," as Jesus told us in the Gospels, you've probably heard His voice, as I have. I've discovered the Lord frequently speaks to us through metaphor (a word or phrase that describes one thing by stating another thing with which it can be compared), analogy (a partial likeness between two things that are compared), and simile (an expression using the words "like" or "as," in which one thing is likened to another that is well known). The Lord has often spoken a rhema word, which was an individual directive just for me, and occasionally, I didn't understand it.

The Lord, who has spoken to me many times, is always the voice of truth. One such example of that occurred when I was a new Christian and also newly married. He said to me one day in prayer, "I've called you to be a vessel of mercy." That is the exact quote. I had no idea what that meant in its personal application to my life. So I searched throughout the Bible for that phrase to gain understanding, and there was no such usage of it to be found. I immediately started searching, researching, and doing Word studies. I love studying God's Word. It's like digging for buried treasure.

Proverbs 25:2 (NKJV) says, **"It is the glory of God**

to conceal a matter but the glory of kings to search it out." I was doing just that!

I quickly learned the New Testament (NT) word for "mercy" is *eleeo*. It is one of the Greek words used for both pity and compassion. In my ignorance, I thought "mercy" was simply a word expressing an emotion, nothing more than a feeling of deep sadness or sorrow for another. As I studied, I realized Jesus was *moved* with compassion or mercy and pity. He exemplified for us that sublime sympathy carries with it responsibility. He did something when He came in contact with someone bound or enslaved by the Devil. Yes, He did something to alleviate their need, captivity, or any form of evil. The word "mercy" in the dictionary says it's a noun, but I would like to suggest it's a verb; it's an action word! To feel mercy toward someone without doing something to remedy his or her situation or circumstance is useless to that individual and to furthering the kingdom of God. So now with clarity and understanding, I believed the Lord wanted me to be one with "eyes to see" and one He could depend on to *do something* when possible and make a difference, in Jesus' name. What you will read in my story is my sincere attempt to be that "vessel of mercy," because I certainly never forgot what He said to me as a baby Christian. All praise and glory to God.

Pearl of Great Price

The parable of the 'pearl of great price' Jesus speaks of in Matthew 13:45–46 says, **"Again the kingdom of heaven is like a merchant seeking beautiful pearls, 46 who when he had found one pearl of great price went and sold all that he had and bought it."**

This parable is teeming with symbolism and speaks of *your* beauty and *your* value in Christ as you express and reflect Him and the kingdom of God. He compares the citizens of His kingdom to that exquisite gem, which is unlike any other. Jesus teaches this parable and it is, therefore, implied that He is the merchant seeking this special treasure. The Hebrew word *c'gullah* (pronounced se-*gul*-lah), means special treasure or jewel, and captures how God sees us; it's revealed in its definition. In this parable, He values that pearl above all else and sells all He has to purchase it and make it His own. Yes, you and I are that pearl, and we were bought at a great price. Jesus paid a high price for this "special treasure." He paid with His life, His blood to purchase you and me. Therefore, we are not our own. If you're His, He sees you as precious, valuable, a special treasure, beautiful, illustrious, and you should be bright, reflecting His light. It is a fact that the most valuable pearls are actually so illustrious they reflect with great clarity the object closest to it. And so should we. The object we are closest to, reflecting as Christians, should be none other than Jesus, the lover of our soul.

The genesis or birth, if you will, of this rare and valuable pearl is analogous to what develops the beauty in us and is both mysterious and miraculous. The birthing of an actual pearl begins with an irritant, such as a piece of sand or a tiny broken piece of shell, that manages to slip inside the closed shell of the oyster. As Christians, we, too, are birthed into the family of God through something small—faith—which is as small as a mustard seed. Faith is meant to be used to develop something incredibly beautiful and valuable in us, as believers, throughout our life.

Many of us come to Christ because of a crisis. Or maybe it's simply an irritant, and we're incapable of getting rid of it ourselves. Whatever the impetus, we realize we need Jesus. Much like the pearl, things we find irritating get under our skin. The oyster slowly begins to develop something uniquely unexplainable around the irritant inside its shell. It releases a transparent, light-infused, crystalline substance that eventually hides and completely covers the unwelcome irritant, making something beautiful of it. As we receive Jesus as Lord and Savior and He births His eternal life and Spirit in us, He begins to develop something exquisitely beautiful in us, as well. It is Christ in us, the hope of glory, the beauty of His character and nature. He changes us from the inside out and takes us from faith to faith and glory to glory. It's an inside job, just like the oyster.

I find it no small coincidence that Jesus compares us to the world-renowned beauty of the pearl. Knowing the origin and the process that created this precious gem makes this comparison meaningful beyond words to the 'pearl of great price' in the parable. First, the market value of each pearl is made up of three distinct variables: its luster, or ability to reflect light, coupled with its inner glow and how well it refracts light and color. This is actually the gem's most important quality. The most valuable pearls reflect the brightest light and with it, a myriad of colors. Second, the valuable pearl should be spotless, without bumps or blemishes. They are considered "clean" if they have no blemishes. Last, the larger the size of the pearl, the more rare and valuable it is. The average, or perfect-sized, pearl is seven millimeters. Seven is the number associated with completion or spiritual perfection in the Bible. There are seven colors in the rainbow, which was manifest in the clouds in the sky when God made His first covenant with humankind. There are also seven continents on the earth, and on those continents lives humankind, made up of every race and color, a virtual rainbow of colors.

One last thing about the pearl needs to be mentioned, pearls are formed in every color, from white to black. No one color is considered more valuable than the other. That is truly a testimony and a beautiful reflection of our great God and His marvelous creation and manifold wisdom. Truly, no detail is too small to be overlooked by Him and He seems to look for unique ways in which He can reflect His character and nature throughout all His creation. As our majestic Creator, we see His beauty and His fingerprints everywhere we look.

When a pearl has fully developed into its most beautiful and magnificent state, it is harvested. One day humankind, created in His image, will also experience a harvest day; it is our final judgment. Jesus is the Lord of our harvest. As Christians, we look forward to that day. It is then that we begin to live eternally in heaven with Jesus, the Bridegroom King, starting with the consummation of the marriage supper of the Lamb. I am ready for that glorious day. Are you ready for the harvest day? Please read Matthew 25:1–13. Five of the ten virgins spoken of in the parable Jesus taught in the wise and foolish virgins were not ready or prepared and could not enter into the room for the wedding. He turned them away, saying, "I do not know you." Please take a moment right now and get right with God. Let it not be said of you that you ignored or rejected the love of Jesus. Who could turn down this free gift? It's the greatest gift ever given to humankind. Think of it, heaven's finest and greatest gift; God's gracious gift of love and forgiveness through simply receiving Jesus Christ as our Lord and Savior as He freely offers eternal life to us all. Why would anyone turn his or her back on such a loving God and Savior? What sane reason exists for that? None, I say, not one.

If you can receive this, you are that pearl of great price that Jesus gave His life for. Are you living for Him, reflecting Him and His light and love? Why not? Peter says in 1 Peter 2:4–5 (NKJV) that we are "living stones."

⁴Coming to Him as to a living stone, rejected indeed by men, but chosen by God and precious, ⁵you also, as living stones, are being built up a spiritual house, a holy priesthood, to offer up spiritual sacrifices acceptable to God through Jesus Christ.

Everything our heavenly Father does or allows in our life is intentional and purposeful, and is meant to bear fruit in our lives. The beautifying or sanctifying process in us as believers requires a faithful commitment to God and "death to self." The death part, that's our job. It's frequently painful, but I urge you to embrace the process. It's worth it. Once you determine to die to self, it's not so painful, because you're dead. Right?

You know that woman we love to hate, the virtuous wife or woman? Proverbs 31:10 says, **"Who can find a virtuous wife? For her worth is far above rubies."** It is written in my *Complete Jewish Bible,* translated by Daniel H. Stern, that the word "rubies" in that verse (Hebrew *Paniyn,* which simply means round) is actually the Hebrew word for pearl. We are compared to pearls in the Old Testament (OT), as well. But our worth "is far above Pearls," said King Solomon, who was nicknamed Lemuel (one of five of his nicknames in the Talmud and the Bible) by his mother, Queen Bathsheba. Isn't it uncanny how similar the lengthy process of creating and beautifying the pearl is to our own beautifying process as His beloved bride?

I beg of you not to reject God's principles or His Word. Read and obey God's Word and be obedient to Him at all costs. His righteousness in our lives comes with great reward. That's precisely why there was such a great price. The reward is, of course, more of Him in you. He is the exceedingly great reward. The price He paid to be one with you, well … He says you're His beloved, and He thinks you're worth it!

Living Lampstands

Through the years, I began to realize the more I prayed and studied God's Word, the more He opened my eyes to see through and with the spirit of revelation. He revealed a spiritual truth to me at one of the lowest times of my life. The depth of that revelation was riveting and literally transformed my thinking regarding tests and trials, and it gave suffering, especially long-suffering, new meaning. I distinctly remember beginning a personal and intense study about the vessels, utensils, and furniture of the tabernacle of meeting, which God instructed Moses to build. I had about six Bible translations along with my lexicons, *Strong's Concordance,* the *Vines Expository Dictionary* and several other commentaries. I sat at my kitchen table for more than twelve hours that day. I studied like that as often as I could. Weekdays were shorter because I homeschooled my daughters. On the weekends, though, Chip sometimes took the girls to the park, or they would play in the backyard together so I could study. I was with them all day during the week, so I didn't feel badly about Chip spending so much time with them when he could.

I was going through an extended season of long-suffering. Over the years in my marriage, I had been forced to become the house police due to my husband's frequent drug use. Chip, my husband, genuinely seemed to hate me and often treated me as though he did. I was keenly aware of the spiritual battle I was engaged in through-out most of my marriage. In addition, I seemed to be surrounded by Job's friends from the OT. I was wildly passionate about Jesus and His Word, and frankly, that's all I talked or thought about. He was my closest and in many ways my only friend. The intimacy of my relationship with Jesus and His Word caused me to actually feel like I lived in another dimension; I called it the *dimension of dominion*. What do I mean by that? I frequently, although not always, knew things before they happened. I understood that as the "mind of Christ," which knows all things (1 Corinthians 2:16).

Unfortunately, during those same years, everywhere I turned were unexplainable and unexpected attacks made up of betrayals, rejection, misunderstandings, and accusations. I'm not good at confrontations, and I refused to defend myself with anyone. God's my Defender, and He said He would also be my rear guard. I depended on Him to do and be that for me. I was well aware that I was greatly misunderstood, I painfully accepted that.

This had been prophesied to me by well-known prophet Kim Clement, when he called me out of the audience and to the platform at a huge meeting many years ago. He spoke of a great women's ministry I would pioneer, but until then, I would be greatly misunderstood, especially in the beginning of my ministry. He paused and then comforted me, saying, "You are in good company … Jesus was misunderstood, too." I was certainly humbled by that comparison.

It was a very long and difficult season, and I frequently felt I was getting "beaten up." That was the phrase in my head. The only safe place for me was in the company of my precious daughters or while I was ministering God's Word. I adored the women in my Proverbs 31 Ministry at the Church on the Way. They understood me, for sure. I was deeply fulfilled in my personal relationship with Jesus and ministering, while teaching women in many different places around Southern California. I had the great honor and privilege of sharing what a living, loving God we serve in Jesus. Daily, He made Himself so real to me. I had many opportunities to teach God's life-giving Word, and nothing compares with that. Still, in many ways I was very alone. It was just me and Jesus.

One day as I was studying the menorah or the golden lampstand in Exodus 25:31–40 (KJV), I read the lampstand was made of pure gold. I knew immediately the pure gold was a picture of and a foreshadowing of Jesus, who was to be and is the Light of the World. The gold represents the purity, the deity of Jesus the Christ, as God. Verse 31 goes on to state the golden lampstand was to be of "beaten work." That's right, it said it was to be *beaten* just as I had been feeling for years – *beaten up*. That phrase meant something deeply personal to me. The visual was powerful. The Holy Spirit was teaching me, using my own words about my situation. Wasn't Jesus *beaten* by the palms of the hands of the Roman soldiers? The entire golden lampstand was to be *of beaten work. Yes, beaten!* My heart actually leapt because I realized for the first time that there was a purpose in the pain I was experiencing and enduring. My suffering was meaningful. All I could hope for was that the character and nature of Jesus was being chiseled into me.

Six branches came out the sides of the *Shamah*, or the central shaft, which represents Jesus, of course. These branches, representing humankind, represent the OT and the NT. We know Eve was birthed from the side of Adam in the Garden of Eden. Then we, His church or body, were birthed out of Jesus's side as the soldier pierced His side (John 19:34), and blood and water came out. The number 6 is the number of humankind. As you know, we were created on the sixth day. In chapter 15 of the book of John, Jesus talks about us being branches in Him, one with Him. Even though there are several different parts that make up the lampstand, it is considered one piece. In Exodus 25:31 the scripture says the golden lampstand consists of the base, its shaft (the center shaft or stem), six branches and shall be of 1 piece. In John 17, known as the High Priestly Prayer, Jesus speaks several times about how we are the branches and are one with God. The golden lampstand in the O.T. Tabernacle is pregnant with symbolism of Jesus, the Light of the World, and His beloved bride or body, the branches.

The lampstand, which was made of approximately seventy-five pounds of pure gold, was considered to be the most beautiful of all the pieces of furniture in the tabernacle, and certainly the most costly. (That lampstand would be worth more than two million dollars today.) Both of these descriptions depict Jesus. The entirety of it was to be beaten into one piece before it could be filled with pure oil. Then it could be lit to give off light or reflect light in front of itself in the Holy Place. That oil represents the infilling of the Holy Spirit. Once it was lit, the Priests were commanded never to let the fire go out (Leviticus 24:1–3). The gold, oil, fire, and light are all emblems of the presence of the Godhead and specifically Jesus, who was to come.

As I began reading Exodus 25 about the golden lampstand and how it was of a beaten work, I knew why I was going through such a difficult time in my life as a Christian, and why I was getting so 'beaten' up. It was truly a life-changing moment for me. I got it. I was a branch *being beaten into shape* and until I was sufficiently beaten, I wouldn't be filled with the fullness of the oil (or His Holy Spirit), give off light, or reflect Him. Since that revelation, I have come to the realization all sacrifice and suffering in Christ are redemptive for me and often others involved in my life. As Christians, we all must endure and overcome trials and hardship. Revelation 3:16 says, "We buy [or trade for] gold refined in the fire." Why had I never heard anyone explain this deep revelation of the golden lampstand before? I've never heard this understanding preached, not even a hint of it.

The light and flame of fire come out of the top of each branch, which is beaten into the shape of a blossom, or as some Bible translations say, a flower or fruit. The final beauty on each stem or branch, representing the believer, seen at the top is the fruit it bears. The light burns from that fruit; even the fruit we bear must go through the fire. Whether your translation says fruit or flower, it's an image that is lovely and beautiful to behold and something we produce by abiding in Christ. We are fulfilling our call and destiny in Christ when our passion for Jesus burns so brightly before others that we become the children of light, seen in the beauty of the fruit we bear.

That fruit that we bear for and in Christ—love, joy, peace, long-suffering, kindness, goodness, faithfulness, gentleness and self-control—do not come easily (Galatians 5:28). Pruning is painful (read John 15). My experience is that it usually comes at great personal cost, learning to die to the flesh, conquering the temptations of the world, and overcoming the Devil's assaults, which come against us as we follow our beloved Savior and learn to love His ways. During this season, I began feeling sorry for myself. He quickly corrected me by speaking a Scripture to me one night. I awoke and ran to open the Bible and read what wonderful thing He just told me. I was sure He felt sorry for me, too. I assure you, He did not. It was Hebrews 5:8 and 11. It reads (I know it by heart), **"Though He was a Son, even He learned obedience by the things which He suffered, of whom we have much to say and hard to explain, since you (me) have become dull of hearing."** He personally rebuked me. I sat crying for hours. Jesus never felt sorry for Himself and takes no pleasure when we feel sorry for ourselves, either. When we do, we actually turn ourselves into our own idol. I repented quickly and set my heart and focus back on Jesus and off myself. He later said to me in another correction during this time, "Long-suffering is a servant to Christ Jesus." I was sufficiently corrected. As a doting daddy, I knew this was His love and mercy toward me. I'm eternally grateful.

Do you actually think you will resemble Christ in character and in the beauty of His nature—and be one with Him—without experiencing hardships, betrayals, and rejections? As I like to say, "Betrayal and rejection are His favorite tools in the toolshed." I've discovered when He gets those out and uses them on me … I've learned to thank God. It proves His love for me.

This was a life changing revelation for me. I recognized in the image of this exquisitely ornate and beautiful 'beaten' golden lampstand, what it meant to me both personally and spiritually. Its incomparable value and illuminating beauty proved why we are privileged to partake in Christ's sufferings. We, too, must be purified, purged and perfected in order to reflect His light forward, symbolized by the lampstand. We embrace hardships and endure trials because of what it produces in us. You think you are going to be like Christ, without being "beaten" into shape? If so, you are sadly mistaken, and so was I. Our bodies are now the temple of God, and He lives within every believer, just as the golden lampstand was within the tabernacle, shedding light and reflecting it forward, as we are commissioned to do, in Christ. That lampstand took quite a beating to be beautified and if you're Christ's, you will, too.

As believers, we are empowered by Jesus and en*light*ened by the indwelling of His Holy Spirit to be children of the light. It all made perfect sense to me. Hardships abound in order to develop His character, His humble nature, and as His branches, to bear much fruit. The light of Christ shines in the heart of every believer, "For God, who commanded light to shine out of darkness, has shone in our hearts to give the light of the knowledge of the glory of God in the face of Jesus Christ" (2 Corinthians 4:6). As His body, we are the heart and hands of Jesus. The kingdom of God is indeed *at hand,* and it begins with yours and mine. Yes, in our hearts and our *hands* - giving God's love away.

I've heard it said to understand is to withstand. Studying the golden lampstand opened my eyes and changed the way I saw my life and my hardships. There is meaning in suffering for Christ's sake. Embrace it and learn from it. I have a much better understanding of the ways of God that beautify us through the analogy of the pearl of great price and how it is developed. A similar principle is at work with the making of the golden lampstand as it was beaten into shape, just as Jesus was beaten on the day He was crucified and punished for my sake. As Christians, we are called to be God's living lampstand, reflecting Jesus Christ in all we say and do. I've ministered this revelation many times now. Every time I do, I see women break down and weep, because they, too, finally have understanding, and their suffering has meaning.

Jesus said in Matthew 11:29–30 (NKJV), [29]**"Take My yoke upon you and learn from Me for I am gentle and lowly in heart and you will find rest for your souls. [30]For My yoke is easy and My burden is light."**

Light. He said His burden is light. In other words, Jesus might say to you, "All I've called you to carry is the weightless burden of My brilliant and radiant light. How heavy can that possibly be?" If you were to light a match in a dark place, how burdensome could that be? Jesus already took the beating, was crucified, and paid the full price to be that Light … to illuminate our darkness. All we have to do is receive His life and His love and reflect Him and His light. Oh, and one more thing; we do have to die daily. But Jesus will help you do that, too, just as He died for you already. The late great Watchman Nee once said, "It is God's great work to reduce us to nothing." Let Him. All the darkness in the world cannot extinguish the light of one candle. It's our job to be that candle.

Go light your world, super-sister-Christian-chic. You and me, we've got a job we've been commissioned to do and to be, because we're His living lampstands. Otherwise, we're nothing more than unprofitable servants.

Proverbs 31:11 (NKJV) says, **"The heart of her husband safely trusts her, so he will have no lack of gain."** Jesus Christ is our Bridegroom King and husband-man. We, as believers, are His beloved bride. His heart safely trusts in us to spread the Word, shine His light, and spread the gospel of Jesus Christ, fulfilling the Great Commission (Mark 16:15–18). He will have no lack of gain as we advance, enforce and increase His kingdom. The Proverbs 31 Scripture was written as a prophetic picture of the coming bride of Christ, His virtuous wife, fulfilling her commission as she, in

His name, works to establish and accomplish the Kingdom of God upon the earth through the hearts and souls of mankind.

Jesus said, **"Let your light so shine before men that they will see your good works and glorify your Father in heaven."** (Matthew 5:16). Amen and Amen.

But you are a chosen generation, a royal priesthood, a holy nation, His own special people, that you may proclaim the praises of Him who called you out of darkness into His marvelous light; 1 Peter 2:9

Shauna Mayer

Jesus said, **"You have heard it said, "You shall love your neighbor and hate your enemy.' 44 "But I say to you, love your enemies, bless those who curse you, do good to those who hate you and pray for those who spitefully use you and persecute you."** Matthew 5:43-44

Shauna as 8 year old

I stood there, a frightened, eight-year-old child, sobbing hysterically in our front yard with my siblings, watching the angry, raging fire burn down our family home. Heroic firefighters and neighbors frantically shoved and carried us out of the range of danger. Random adults tried to assure me in the midst of this chaos that "everything is going to be okay" but, I did not believe that. What was I thinking? That nothing would ever be the same again. I was right.

That exceptionally hot August afternoon in Houston, Texas, is one I'll never forget. The overwhelming smell of smoke, the sound of crackling wood, the sight of red-and-gold dancing flames, and the extreme heat are forever etched in my mind. The temperature that afternoon was oppressive; not one child could be found playing outside. Of course, that all changed in an instant when the fire trucks, with their loud sirens, came screaming down Kenilwood Street to the Sullivan house, which was engulfed in flames.

That afternoon was the beginning of a series of awful and unforeseen events that completely changed the course of our family's lives. I praise God that no lives were lost that day and that no one was even hurt. We lost absolutely everything, though. The fire started in the garage. The arson investigators were not able to trace the exact origin or reason for the fire, so it has remained a mystery. We had nothing left but the clothes each of us put on that morning.

As you can imagine, that day is one of the most emotional and vivid memories of my life. I distinctly remember grieving over the thought of my beloved Thumbelina doll burning up in the fire, along with my brand-new brass bed, which I had just received as a birthday present weeks before. Both had special meaning to me and were valued treasures. As I stood helplessly watching the raging fire burn down our home, I cried with an abandon I'd never known before. I was deeply traumatized.

Just Give Me Jesus

Even at that tender age, I had a deep, abiding love and devotion to Jesus. As a family, we did not go to church regularly, although we went often enough so I knew who Jesus was. I also knew He loved me and was told He knew me by name. Knowing that somebody loved me, especially Jesus, was very important to me. I knew Him as the Son of God and the Savior of the world. He was already my Savior and closest friend.

My parents were nice enough people. There was no incest, and no one was beaten or any such thing, but there was no love in our home. The lack of love and affection in my childhood made me hunger and thirst after Jesus all the more.

Sunday School and Jesus

As a little girl, attending Sunday school was the highlight of my life. I waited all week for Sunday, hoping we would go to church that morning. I remember my excitement and running to class, not so much to be on time, but so I could sit in the front seat in the first row. That way, nothing could escape my little ears or eyes about my beloved Jesus.

Early on, Jesus was the love of my life, and I considered Him my best friend. He was always on my mind, and I secretly talked to Him all day long. My desire even then was to please Him. Today I would say I wanted my life to bring Him glory. I distinctly remember telling my friends, "You can be perfect, you know, if you have Jesus in your heart." In every decision I made, even when wondering whether to tattle on a brother or sister, I would seriously consider, "What would Jesus do?"

Just prior to our house fire, I had a visitation from Jesus in my backyard, while playing on our swing set. He stood before me and told me several key things that would occur in my life. He also told me about a few people (He mentioned no names) and things I should avoid. Today, all but one has come to pass. His last point was something specific about me. I believe what He spoke had to do with the calling on my life to share the good news of the gospel of Jesus Christ and to prove that He is real.

My visitation with Jesus occurred just weeks before my eighth birthday. Our house caught fire only a few weeks later. To this day, I wholeheartedly believe the Lord revealed Himself to me to strengthen me for the awful events that lay ahead. And strengthen me it did. In my little heart and mind, I knew Jesus loved me, so almost nothing else mattered.

Innocence Lost

During the rebuilding of our home, we stayed in a nearby hotel that had larger, apartment-type rooms for extended stays. One afternoon, while swimming in the hotel pool, I met a nice little girl my age. We became fast friends, and she asked me to spend that night with her. I excitedly asked my parents, and to my surprise, they said yes.

After I got to her room, I remember watching her mother (a divorced woman) getting dressed up to leave. We had already put on our pajamas and were lying in separate twin beds, watching TV. Soon after her mother left, we both dozed off to sleep, alone.

I was abruptly awakened when I realized someone was in bed with me, taking off my pajamas. I later learned he was my friend's eighteen-year-old brother. He had a friend with him, who was standing beside my bed, watching. They both performed oral sex on and had intercourse with me as I lay there, crying and paralyzed with fear. My biggest fear was that they were going to kill me. I silently cried though the terrible ordeal, but I quietly and fearfully submitted.

My friend's brother was the initiator. The other young man did not want to participate, but my friend's brother bullied him into it. Although hesitant, he followed the urging of his friend and sexually assaulted me, too.

My little friend slept soundly throughout the night, and no parent came to my rescue. However, God saw it all, and through an unexpected event, my parents soon found out about my rape.

Several days later, as I walked down the Hotel hallway, those same young men grabbed me and pulled me into an empty hotel room, attempting a repeat performance of that awful night. I stood there, scared, trembling, crying, saying no, and begging them to leave me alone. Just then the hotel manager happened to walk past the room and heard voices and knowing it was supposed to be vacant, he unexpectedly opened the door to investigate. When he burst in, he saw me crying. He confronted the two young men and quickly escorted me out of the room. I had been rescued! The manager called the police and then told my parents. God divinely intervened.

Police, Doctors, and Attorneys

This began humiliating meetings with police, doctors, attorneys, and others and many embarrassing, probing questions. Eventually, the courtroom proceedings began. The first trial went by quickly and the friend of my friend's older brother was found guilty and was sentenced and incarcerated. The family of the instigator hired a high-profile, prominent, criminal defense attorney from Houston, Percy Foreman, who was called the "King of the Courtroom." He later would defend James Earl Ray, who assassinated Martin Luther King, Jr., and would become one of America's best-known trial lawyers.

There were two separate trials—one for each man involved in my sexual assault. Soon after the sentencing of the first young man, the second trial began with Percy Foreman. By this time, I was filled with embarrassment and paralyzed with shame. I was horrified that I had to go through all that again, sitting in court, alone in that big witness chair, talking about what had happened. I cried often. It was a terrible chapter in my life. I prayed to Jesus a lot.

I learned early in life how to lean on and depend on the Lord. I believe He empowered me and was with me throughout that horrible ordeal.

The Second Trial

The second trial was much more memorable than the first because of Percy Foreman. I have vivid memories of this ruthless character cross-examining me on the witness stand. I was crying so hard I could no longer speak. I'm sure I wasn't older than ten at the time. Embarrassed and sobbing, I tried to find words to explain what those men did to me. I said they had, "put their pee-pee into my pee-pee." I was sobbing so hard at that point the judge hammered the gavel, stopped the proceedings, and with a loud voice called a recess. I remember my daddy verbally threatening to kill someone with a gun in the hallway and then all the resulting commotion.

I was told my parents were then advised to drop the second case due to the attention and publicity it was receiving in Houston, not to mention the damage it was doing to me. I thank God my parents agreed and dropped the case, although I believe they were reluctant and angry. Sadly, the one who initiated that despicable crime walked free, while the other had to serve time in prison.

So much heartache was done to my parents (I imagine they silently blamed themselves for my rape), our family, and me since the house fire and my sexual assault. I have no doubt there must have been a great deal of anger and confusion about how to handle me after learning of my rape. But no one ever spoke with me or comforted me—not a parent, a pastor, or a qualified counselor. No one helped give this eight-year-old girl understanding or insight or guided me through this painful and traumatic ordeal, much less show me how to overcome it. However, as I look back at those traumatic events, the timing and the sequence of the Lord revealing Himself to me and speaking to me strengthened me for those awful experiences. I'm amazed at the deep personal relationship I shared with Jesus as a little girl. It fortified me in a supernatural way.

I realize now, I taught myself coping skills. I would not allow myself to think about what happened to me but only to think happy thoughts and anticipate things I was looking forward to. I never discussed it with anyone. Thank goodness, I didn't blame myself. I knew I had done nothing to provoke those sexual assaults, so at least I had no guilt associated with it. I taught myself, through this experience, how to cope with difficulty. I became very resilient.

As a Christian adult, I marveled when I first read that very thing in Philippians 4:8, **"Finally, brethren, whatever things are true, whatever things are noble, whatever things are just, whatever things are pure, whatever things are lovely, whatever things are of good report, if there is any virtue, if there is anything praiseworthy-meditate on these things."** That's exactly what I had done.

Always Looking over My Shoulder

After those initial rapes, I also experienced other sexual attacks and attempted rapes as I grew up. It's been an ongoing assignment I've had to deal with throughout my life. I'm always looking over my shoulder. Due to those experiences, I am extremely protective of my two daughters at all times. I cannot stress enough to parents about the importance of making wise and informed decisions regarding the whereabouts of your children. It is our duty to preserve and protect their innocence. We are accountable to God, how we guard, guide, and protect our little ones. I take that responsibility very seriously. I recommend that every mother and father do the same. That's your job!

Shooting Snakes

Immediately after moving into our newly rebuilt home, my parents, having just learned about my rape, quickly sold it. We moved just outside the Houston city limits to a sparsely populated rural area. It consisted of nothing more than cow pastures, cows, and rice canals.

We lived between two rice canals, on a dirt/shell road with virtually no neighbors, but surrounded by snakes. Poisonous Water Moccasins love water and they seemed to be everywhere. One of my favorite pastimes during the summer was taking my brother's 12-gauge shotgun and walking up the road to the water canal and shooting snakes. I was a good shot, too. I remember killing so many one afternoon, that when I returned to the canal a couple of days later, it reeked with the smell of their rotting dead bodies floating on the surface of the water. Miranda Lambert's got nothing over me!

Today, the weapons of my warfare are no longer guns, but pleading the blood of Jesus, using the authority we have in the name of Jesus and praying the Word of God to annihilate and destroy all demonic enslavement, evil strongholds and every attack against myself and others. That includes all the 'snakes' and enemies of our soul that try and slither into our lives to bring deception, destruction and death. There's power in the name of Jesus!

Done with Church

After we moved, my mother had no desire to attend church any longer. I distinctly remember begging her to take me to church on many different occasions, but she wouldn't. From then on, we had no affiliation with a church, Christians, or the Lord. We never spoke of or referred to any of the crises that led us to move away from everyone to the middle of nowhere. She wanted to forget it ever happened. It wasn't quite that easy for me.

My Home Life

I was raised in a home with a great deal of discipline (now I am extremely grateful for that) and absolutely no affection or expression of love. My mother was the dominant force in our home, and she was indeed a force to be reckoned with. She wasn't a very happy person, and I always had the feeling she didn't like being a mother and we children were a bother. I have no memory of a hug or a kiss or even an encouraging word. I was the middle child and usually overlooked. My mother favored two of her four children, and I was not one of those two. I learned to accept the indifference and rejection at home. I didn't feel sorry for myself; it's much easier to simply accept the things you are powerless to change.

I became the cheerleader or the peacemaker in the family when it was needed. I didn't complain or share my opinion; it wouldn't be listened to or valued anyway (I've also learned keeping your opinions to yourself is a good and godly thing, too). Nevertheless, my life outside the home was quite remarkable. Only God could have given me the grace and favor with my peers that I had throughout school. I was amazed and humbled at how my friends and classmates would elect or select me for the highest honors.

I would never think to run for or compete for any titles because of my lack of self-confidence. Deep down I was shy and painfully insecure. What offset those deficits in my personality was the fact I really loved and enjoyed people. That caused me to care for others and helped me overcome my shyness.

From kindergarten through the third grade, while we still lived in Houston, the local Little League boys baseball team selected me as their "Team Sweetheart." I loved that! Throughout elementary and middle school, much to my surprise, I was consistently selected as the most popular or most beautiful girl in class. When I entered high school, we moved to Alvin (which is part of the Houston, Woodlands, and Sugarland Metropolitan area) located about halfway between Houston and Galveston and 30 miles from the rural area where we had been living. It was a very large 4-A school. I was selected most beautiful in the high school, "Miss Alvin High School," Homecoming Queen, County Queen, and on and on. I was always shocked when they announced my name as the winner. It was much more meaningful to me in light of how unpleasant my home life was.

Miss Brazoria County

My last title, "Miss Brazoria County" (the birthplace of the Republic of Texas) qualified me to run for Miss Texas, which I was greatly encouraged to do. I declined the opportunity, feeling strongly that whatever caused me to be well liked by my peers certainly wasn't physical beauty. I knew there was nothing special about me; there were much more beautiful girls in school than I was. I always thought it had something to do with the presence of Jesus in my life. I truly believe it was the light of His love shining through me, nothing more. Therefore, although encouraged by others, I never entered local or state beauty contests.

Touched by an Angel

The summer I turned fourteen was another memorable birthday. I was "touched by an angel" while vacationing with my best friend and her mother in Acapulco. I ventured down the beach by myself, after my friend had fallen asleep on the sand. The turquoise color of the waters was so beautiful, so inviting, and it was a very hot day. I noticed no one was swimming in the ocean. Now I realize the locals knew better than to go in the water that day. The waves looked pretty big but not dangerous, and certainly not life threatening.

I jumped in and swam out just a short bit before I got sucked out by a huge wave. Immediately, this mighty wave came crashing down around me and threw me to the bottom of the ocean floor. The waves were so rough and violent I couldn't find my way to the top to take a breath of air. I was tossed around like a rag doll. It was all happening so fast. I was fighting the waves, fighting for air, and ultimately, fighting for my life. The big, powerful waves kept tossing me around and throwing me to the ocean floor. I had no strength and was quickly giving up. I was incapable of saving myself and becoming lifeless. I knew I was going to drown; I was actually going to die.

As soon as I completed that thought, two strong hands came out of nowhere. They immediately found me and pulled me up and out of the deep and turbulent waves and straight up in the air. *What's happening?* I wondered. *Who could this be, lifting me up in the air, high above the deep waters and the tall waves? How big must he be?* Suddenly, my limp body was carried to the shore. I was too weak to open my eyes to see who was saving me. Not a single word was spoken as he gently laid me down on the sand. Wasn't it odd that he didn't ask how I was? Then the one who saved my life silently walked away and left me. I couldn't move; I still had no strength. I think I may have laid there an hour or two, completely weak and disheveled. My bathing suit was coming off, and sand was everywhere and my body was aching. I felt like I had been beaten up. My long hair, which was almost to my waist, looked like a bird's nest. When I finally came to, there was no one within eyesight. Not a single person.

I had a sense of the great size and strength of the one who

carried me through those deep and rough waters. Even in my semiconscious state, I marveled at the way he walked through the deep and conquered the turbulent waters, his body steady and unmoved by the mighty strength and power of those huge waves. That day, my life was sovereignly saved by almighty God and the holy angelic host He sent for me. My experience was featured in a 2 hour TBN movie many years ago entitled, "Angel's, God's Miraculous Messengers."

Isaiah 43:1–3 says,

"Fear not for I have redeemed you, I have called you by your name; you are Mine. When you pass through the waters I will be with you; and through the rivers, they will not overflow you. When you walk through the fire, you shall not be burned, nor shall the flame scorch you. For I am the Lord your God. The Holy One of Israel, your Savior."

College Cheerleading

As a college cheerleader, there was not a double stunt I couldn't do with my partner. I did flips in the air, jumps and flips off his shoulders, round-offs, wraparounds, the splits. It was the passion of my life. I was a high school cheerleader and went on to became a cheerleader at Texas Tech University in Lubbock, which I attended in my freshman year. I transferred to North Texas State University in Denton for my sophomore year, immediately became a cheerleader there. I had an opportunity to cheer that year in the Dallas Cowboy Stadium. That was a memorable experience.

By my junior year, I was tired of college and ready to step into a career. I wanted to travel and see the world.

New York City, New York

I was hired by American Airlines and graduated from their flight school in Dallas in April of '76. There were about fifty flight attendants in the class, and a girl named Kris Houghton and

I became fast friends. After graduating we were both based in New York City, with many other classmates. Kris and I both got transferred to LA about eight months later. Kris, two fellow flight attendants, and I rented a fabulous penthouse apartment in Brentwood, California. My friend Kris later married and became Mrs. Kris Kardashian. You would know her today as Mrs. Kris Jenner. I marvel at how differently our lives have unfolded since our days together as flight attendants.

Los Angeles RAMS Cheerleader

Shauna as L.A. RAMS Cheerleader
at 1980 SUPERBOWL

I quit flying a few months after moving to LA and quickly became a working TV actress and a model. In 1978 I also became an original LA Rams cheerleader. Over one thousand young women tried out the first year, and twenty-four of us were selected. I cheered for two years. The second year, the Rams went to the Super Bowl in Pasadena, where they played the Pittsburgh Steelers. We were ahead the first three quarters, but the Steelers went ahead in the fourth, and won the game 31–19. It was one of the greatest experiences of my life, cheering in front of 103,100 people and on live TV around the world. As cheerleaders, we did a Bob Hope

Super Bowl special in January. Life appeared to be wonderful, didn't it?

Television Actress

My years as a cheerleader were lots of fun. I made some great friends on the squad, since we spent so much time together at rehearsal and doing personal appearances, commercials, magazine ads and such. But it was the beginning of many empty and lost years. As an actress, I appeared in many episodes of television series such as *Fantasy Island, Love Boat,* and *Charley's Angels.* I was John Ritter's girlfriend in *Three's Company.* I also did several screen tests and shot many TV pilots during those years.

Unfortunately, over the last ten years, I had slowly begun to forget about Jesus. I may not have looked like it, but I felt empty and lost. Thank God, Jesus came to save that which was lost (Matthew 18:11).

Dating always seemed to be a disappointment, too. My boyfriend in high school and throughout college was a football quarterback. After five years of dating, I broke up with him when I moved to New York. Now as an adult, my boyfriends were famous NFL quarterbacks, and MLB pitchers. Each one was a serious celebrity featured in stories and on covers for magazines such as *Sports Illustrated.* They were used to being chased by fans, mostly women. From the time I was twenty-two years old until I met my husband, I dated in succession, four professional athletes. Each was completely caught up in his fame and not seeking any real commitment. I shouldn't have been dating these types of men because I knew on some level they were all players. All were unfaithful. Not a Christian in the group. But, of course, at that time I wasn't living like a Christian, either. Regardless of how each relationship ended, it left me questioning my self-worth and depleted my self-esteem. So what did I do after each break up? I dusted myself off, found myself another incredibly successful and famous athlete, and started over.

What's a Psychic?

It was at this same time in my life that I was invited—begged—by a roommate to go with her to see a psychic. I didn't even know what that word meant—"psychic." Don't forget, I grew up in "small-town" Texas. We don't have psychics there. We had rednecks, bull riders, cowboys, and lots of horses, cows, and snakes. But I had never met or heard of a psychic.

I remember getting a funny feeling in the pit of my stomach when invited. I didn't want to go, but she pressed. So I went with her to see the tea leaves' reader. Because of the lack of God in my life, I was ignorant to the ways of the Devil and was vulnerable and easily deceived. This psychic was actually pretty accurate about my life, and although at first I found that confusing, I soon became a big advocate of all that darkness and deception, which also bordered on the New Age Movement. I knew nothing about the spirit realm and was convinced what was spoken to me came directly from God. Who else could know my past, present, and future so well? The kingdom of darkness and familiar spirits, that's who. I wish I'd known that truth then. Please read; Leviticus 19:31, 20:6, Deuteronomy 18:9-13.

In my ignorance, I refused to believe in a Devil. I thought some people were evil and others, needing to blame their bad or criminal behavior on someone, simply made up this "Devil" idea. I'm sure you've heard the saying, "The greatest trick the Devil ever pulled was convincing the world he didn't exist." I subscribed to that school of thought. I've heard it said that approximately 30% of the recorded ministry of Jesus in the 4 Gospels was praying for and casting out demons (or unclean spirits) out of people. Demons are indeed very real. Read the Bible.

God warns us to stay away from sorcerers, magicians, astrologers, and prognosticators. Those are some of the names in the Bible of people filled with the Devil who try to advise you or tell your future. They fall under the category of "fortune-tellers." These people are full of the Devil and deception, and whether they know it or not, they're lying to you. Involvement with these individuals opens spiritual doors in your life to the kingdom of darkness and can give place to destruction and possibly even death, if the devil has his way. The Bible calls this divination and is definitely not of God or anything good. Satan uses these devices to steal, kill, and destroy us.

As I said, God warns us throughout the Bible to stay away from them. Of course, I didn't know that then, because I didn't read the Bible. I was thoroughly convinced the knowledge psychics received from astrology and reading tea leaves, palms, tarot cards, and so on came directly from God. I was deceived and completely ignorant to the schemes and plans of the Devil. Remember, after eight years of age, I had no further knowledge of Jesus or the Word of God. I was an easy target for the Devil. Soon after that psychic reading, I was hooked. I started going to every psychic, astrologist, numerologist, and graphologist I could find and afford. Lost and empty, I was desperately seeking something. I was disillusioned with life and unfulfilled most of the time. I was convinced all I needed was a better psychic. **"My people are destroyed for lack of knowledge"** (Hosea 4:6).

By the way, I never found a better psychic. Why? Because they're **ALL** liars and deceivers! It's important for me to share, that since then, I have confessed, renounced and repented for my ignorance and involvement in all forms of fortune-telling and divination. I have turned from all that divination and fully turned to God. Read 1 John 1:9.

Who Is Kendra Elaine Cubbison?

When I was twenty-five years old and in the middle of those years of confusion, I accidentally uncovered a well-kept family secret during a trip to Texas for my sister's wedding. While going through some legal papers in our family home, I discovered adoption papers with my name on them. The document said my name at birth was Kendra Elaine Cubbison, which was later changed to

Susan Elaine Sullivan. My name was Kendra until I was about two years old. Was I confused!

I found out my biological father had left my mother, older brother, and myself when I was only about eighteen months old. My young parents soon divorced. Supported by her parents, my mother, brother, and I moved to a small apartment next door to a wonderful man named Donald Sullivan. They met, fell in love, and married soon after. He legally adopted my older brother and I and changed our names. My mother had two more children with Donald Sullivan. Because we were so young, we had no memory of our first family. Stumbling upon the adoption papers rocked my world and resulted in a bit of an identity crisis.

I have since looked up and met my biological father, and he is a really nice man. But Mr. Sullivan is my *real* dad, though. Unfortunately, as children we didn't see much of him. He always worked two jobs and never complained about it. He is one of the kindest, most caring people I've ever known. His kindness had a profound effect on my life. He had a genuine concern for others, especially those in need. I never knew or suspected he wasn't my real dad. I am here to testify that blended families can work. Wonderful stepparents are certainly out there. Donald Sullivan was the best part of my childhood, and I will always be grateful to God for him.

Named after Shaun Cassidy

At this point you may be wondering where the name Shauna came from. When I started acting and was eligible to become a member of the Screen Actors Guild (SAG), I was told there were three other Susan Sullivan's in the SAG union. I was forbidden to join using my name. I had to change either my first or last name. I was so angry about being forced to change my name that I refused to do anything about for a few months.

Some time later, my agent called and sent me out to read for a part playing the love interest of actor Shaun Cassidy. I didn't get the part. I did get a new name, though. I loved Shaun's name and thought, *if I must change my name, Shauna is as good as any.* I liked that it was uncommon. Hollywood! Since then I have grown to love it, especially after learning Shauna is a derivative of Hannah in the Bible, which means favored or gracious.

Meeting and Marrying Chip Mayer, 1987-2006

On December 19, 1987, I was at a "Hollywood-type" Christmas party. It was sponsored by the modeling agency I was listed with and held at an enormous Beverly Hills mansion owned by a world famous movie star. The movie star wasn't there that night, but my future husband was.

Wow! As I stood in the room where all the food was laid out, nibbling on hors d'oeuvres, the world stopped for just a moment as I noticed the most perfect specimen of a man I had ever seen. As he walked into the room, I couldn't stop staring at him. He didn't look real; he looked more like a Greek god, tall, dark, and handsome. Or maybe I should say beautiful. He was! He walked over and stood to the right of me, where I stood, still staring at him. Then he lit up a cigarette. *Ugh,* I thought, *that is so gross! How could a guy like that smoke?* I leaned over to him and said flirtatiously, "Didn't anybody tell you it's no longer cool to smoke?" He leaned back over to me and said, "I don't give a —!" My mouth fell open. I stood there stunned he had spoken to me like that. He turned and walked out of the room. *Well,* I thought, *he sure told me!*

Within a few minutes, he walked back in the room and straight over to me. He began apologizing profusely and introduced himself as Chip Mayer. Again, I was taken off guard because this time he was personable and sincere. He seemed so normal. He invited me on a private tour of the mansion with him, as if it were his. I was a bit hesitant, but I joined him and we toured the mansion together.

I soon discovered he was brilliantly funny and unbelievably quick-witted. I actually got cramps in my cheeks laughing that night. I remember laughing so hard I had tears streaming down my face. Could this be my Prince Charming? He sure looked the part.

We started dating right away. Chip actually proposed marriage on our first date. We were at a restaurant, and he got down on one knee in front of my chair and asked me to marry him. He was holding a cigar band in his hand and slipped it on my finger. It was flattering and a little awkward, but I laughed and again wondered if he was the "one." A proposal on the first date—now that was a first! He would continue to propose every day, every date, and every night for the next two years, until I eventually said yes!

Chip Was Different

Chip was different than anyone I had ever dated. He chain-smoked, drank, cussed, and frequently did drugs. I have always thought of myself as simple and a bit square. I'd never smoked, rarely drink, and I've never been interested in drugs. So his lifestyle and choices were unlike mine. But like many women, I thought I could change him. It wouldn't be so hard. I was up for the challenge, and I believed Chip was worth it.

James Dean and Pollyanna

I was soon intoxicated with love, and Chip's destructive James Dean lifestyle was rather exhilarating and fun. He made me feel alive. I was the typical "good girl" attracted to the "bad boy." There were many red flags I should have noticed, especially in the beginning, but I looked the other way. I've heard it said that "Once you get emotionally involved with a man, it's like Novocaine to the brain." It was true for me.

We fell deeply in love ... or was it lust or both? He was thirty-three years old when we met and had been married and divorced twice already. He was raising his four-year-old daughter. Due to the divorce with her mother, he was riddled with guilt and self-destructive and undisciplined, as was his daughter. She did not like me at all and wanted nothing to do with me. She made that clear up front. She wanted her daddy all to herself. I couldn't blame her!

True to my Pollyanna personality, though, I believed she would quickly grow to love me. I wasn't worried about it.

The X-Wives

I quickly met the mother of his daughter who was also an actress, but I didn't know who she was and had never heard of the TV show she had been on, either. That probably made it much easier for us to be friends. She was just Chip's first x-wife. I liked her and I made every effort to be a good friend to her through the years. We became close Christian sisters in the Lord. Chip and his second wife had just divorced a few months before we met. She was the HUGE Soap Opera star at the time and still is. I didn't even watch Soap Operas and I knew who she was. You couldn't walk through a grocery store without seeing her beautiful face on a few different covers. I was actually a fan of hers and had a few of those magazines in my apartment when Chip and I met. I was stunned to discover that was his most recent wife. I have to admit, I felt intimidated by her beauty and success but, their relationship was completely over. I never had a chance to meet her until Chip's Memorial service in 2011. She was very gracious to attend that day.

The Soap Opera Santa Barbara

When Chip and I met he was part of the cast of the NBC soap opera *Santa Barbara*. T. J. Daniels was his character's name. Coincidentally, he was the "bad boy" on the soap, too. I'd never seen it and didn't recognize him as an actor, because I rarely watched TV. He had phenomenal success from the moment he moved from New Jersey to L.A. From motion pictures to starring in commercials, movies of the week, and pilots, and guest starring roles, as well as replacing Tom Wopat in the wildly popular prime time TV show *The Dukes of Hazards,* he was, by all Hollywood standards, a very successful actor.

Chip as Vance Duke on "Dukes of Hazards"

Though, he was troubled in some ways, he was also a very caring and sensitive boyfriend - when he was sober. I believed Chip to be deeply emotionally wounded due to the 2 failed marriages he'd gone through in the last 5 years and I assumed that's why he escaped into drugs and alcohol. I remember thinking, *Aren't we all emotionally wounded?* The difference is most of us tried to cope with and work out our issues, not drown them in alcohol and drugs, which Chip did. That was the problem.

I believed I could love Chip enough to make him realize his worth and value as a person and get him to kick his bad habits. Knowing nothing about addictive substances such as alcohol or drugs, I had no idea what I was getting involved with. Regardless of what he did, I was determined to get him healed and delivered from those bad habits. Or were they demons? I was beginning to wonder...

Living in Sin

As we continued to date, Chip was also, repeatedly asking me to move in with him. I lived at the beach, and I absolutely loved it. I jogged and biked every day by the water. Physical exercise was one of my great passions. He lived in Sherman Oaks (which is in Los Angeles County), close to NBC Studios. Eventually I moved in with him. I had never lived with a boyfriend before. Both morally and spiritually, I knew it was wrong, but I justified it by convincing myself that as soon as he quit all his bad habits, we would get married. He put a big beautiful ring on my finger, and we were officially engaged and <u>living in sin</u>...*and I knew it.*

When you're sinning and you know it, you keep waiting for that lightning bolt from heaven to come down and zap you. When it doesn't happen, you actually think you're getting away with it. Don't be fooled. God sees everything we do and knows everything about us and He loves us anyway. 2 Peter 3:9c says, **"He is not willing that any should perish but that all should come to repentance."** God is long suffering and patient with us, hoping we'll notice His goodness toward us and will choose Him and His merciful kindness over our sin. That's how loving and gracious our heavenly Father is. It's the goodness of God that leads us to repentance. He is faithful to us even when we are not faithful to Him. Why? Because Jesus loves sinners, and we're all sinners who need a Savior. Jesus is the One and only Savior.

After I moved in with Chip, I noticed he wasn't making any attempts to end his substance abuse, although he gave Oscar-winning performances trying to convince me otherwise. He was an actor, an especially good actor when it came to protecting his alcohol and drug habits. Why wouldn't he just stop smoking, drinking, and doing cocaine? Why didn't he just stop? I didn't understand. Why all the lies and broken promises? It couldn't be that difficult! Every day and every time he got drunk or high,

Chip said it was "the last time." He seemed so genuine each time he promised me that. I believed him every single time, too. I was so naïve.

Chip Was Crippled

Everything in Chip's life—absolutely everything—had come easily. He came from a loving, wonderful, wealthy family back east. He was the eldest of seven beautiful, adoring children. He was raised in a Norman Rockwell print.

Intellectually, he was brilliant. And if that wasn't enough, he had a bona fide photographic memory. For instance, he could memorize five pages of dialogue by reading through his script once or twice in the car on the way to NBC each morning. They were often monologues. I was blown away by that. Physically, he was big, almost 6'3" and worked out daily with weights. He was incredibly lean and strong, with muscles that made him look like a bodybuilder. I'm not exaggerating. His personality was dazzling, and his good looks were unforgettable … intimidating really.

But emotionally he was crippled. Chip had acquired no coping skills in the course of his life because in Chip Mayer's life, he hadn't experienced hardship. This was in direct contrast to my life, where I had to teach myself coping skills to deal with the injustices of life as far back as I could remember.

Chip quickly recognized my inner strength. Although he said he admired it and was drawn to it, he was frequently irritated that I was able to deal with unpleasant situations and people so easily, including him and all his nonsense. He didn't understand me, my resilience, and my innate ability to calmly and maturely handle hardships. I think he eventually grew to resent me because of it. He couldn't relate to it at all.

Hollywood Is a Heartbreaker

Hollywood will eat you up and spit you out. So although Chip worked a lot, he also was rejected quite a bit, too. As an actor you can't take it personal, that's typically the way the entertainment business works. There are LOTS of interviews and LOTS of rejection. The Casting Directors know what they're looking for before you walk in the door and you're either 'it' or you're not. I experienced it, too. So, Chip's great escape became his alcohol and his drugs when he couldn't cope. I eventually came to the conclusion that he enjoyed doing drugs and frequently told me when he was drunk or high that he felt, "invisible, ten feet tall, and bulletproof." He wasn't kidding.

Born Again

After I moved in with Chip and realized his unbridled lust for and use of alcohol and cocaine weren't decreasing, as he'd promised, I decided if he didn't clean up his act, I would have to break our engagement and move out. I told him so.

Through my experiences and those I've witnessed with others, most often it's personal crises that bring us to Christ. That was the case with Chip and me. When Chip's destructive choices weren't changing, I suddenly remembered my first love, Jesus Christ. I knew Jesus could save Chip from himself. I thought if I could just get him saved (see John 3:16), Jesus would set him free from the addictions, and I could marry him. I believed we could live happily ever after.

So that's what I did. I took him with me to a nearby church. And lo and behold, he received Jesus as Lord and got radically saved that day. Chip was so ready and so eager to give his life over to Jesus. He was tired of doing things his way. We both were born again, as the Scripture says (John 3:3–8). Chip and I fell deeply in love with Jesus Christ together and were filled with joy and hope for our future.

Crying, Sweating, Shaking, and Trembling

We began to attend the Church on the Way regularly, where we got saved. We both loved attending church services and learning about Jesus. We also learned together what it meant to be a Christian.

In the beginning, I actually believed we were the only sinners there at the Sunday services. So in order not to pollute the other saints in the sanctuary, we'd kind of sneak into the back row of the large East Campus sanctuary, hoping no one would notice us and recognize that we were sinners. They all looked so perfect from behind. In my mind, if they actually realized how imperfect we were, they might actually ask us to leave or worse still, stone us right there. I know now we're all sinners saved by Gods' great grace.

We'd sit at the back and though we understood very little about the sermon, we'd both cry. Chip would actually tremble and sweat. We quickly felt the presence and power of the Holy Spirit under the teaching and pastoral leadership of Pastor Jack Hayford. The Holy Spirit was transforming both our lives. We were hungry for God—more like sponges, soaking in the Word and learning of His great love for us.

We immediately bought a Bible, our first beloved Bible. How we treasured it. Then I purchased a Christian dictionary, so I could look up unfamiliar words Pastor Jack used in the Sunday morning sermon. I'd write down all the words I didn't know while he preached and looked them up as soon as we got home. There were a lot of them. We had a lot to learn.

I Was Lost, but now I'm Found

I actually thought I was a Christian when I first took Chip to church, while we were living in sin and having sex together. After we started going to church, I realized being a Christian means much more than simply hearing and knowing about Jesus. He must be your personal Savior and the Lord of your life. As the saying goes, "I didn't realize how lost I was until I was found."

Ironically, while trying to save Chip, I was radically saved myself. When we met, I had spiritually backslidden and was in a very confused state. Much of this can be traced to the fortune-telling deception I became involved with.

I got so convicted about us living together in sin—the Bible calls it fornication (that's any sexual involvement outside of marriage) and sexual immorality—that I moved out and moved back to the beach! I loved Jesus so much that I didn't want to grieve Him; I wanted to please Him. I wanted to live a pure and holy life. I had a burning desire to be obedient and loyal to Him in all things. The truth is I loved Jesus more than I loved Chip.

Posers and Pretenders

Chip was getting convicted, too, but in the meantime, we were living separately. He called people who claimed to be Christians, but lived a different way behind closed doors, "posers and pretenders." I did not want to be one of those types of Christians.

When I moved out, it rocked his world. That definitely got his attention! He then made the choice to quit everything destructive. He finally exercised self-control and let go of all his bad habits. Chip began to treat me and date me in a Christian fashion. We were no longer engaged in any sexual behavior and remained abstinent until we were married.

We spent our time together reading the Bible out loud to one other and praying. It was wonderful. We were growing in the Lord and never happier. My respect and love for Chip skyrocketed to a new high. I fell in love all over again because he was a new man.

We'd been dating for almost two years now, and he kept proposing marriage. I kept waiting and watching to see if he was going to slip and fall off the wagon. He remained clean and sober, and after many months, when I was thoroughly convinced that he was indeed a new man, I finally said yes. We secretly made plans to go to Vegas and elope the next weekend. I couldn't tell my friends, because I knew they would all try to talk me out of it.

I finally believed he was delivered, and we were to be married. In November 1989, we secretly married. I was elated, and so was he.

Falling off the Wagon

Chip got drunk the night we got married. I was shocked, stunned, and felt stupid. I was scared that I had waited two years to marry him, and the very thing I feared was already back. *How could I have been so deceived?* I was completely blindsided by his choice to drink again. Regardless, I took my vows and covenant with Chip—and God—very seriously. A 3-fold cord would NOT be easily broken in my life and furthermore, I have never been a "quitter."

The bottom fell out of our marriage right away. Chip was no longer working on the soap opera. He wasn't told why, but they wrote him out of the show many months before. I presume it was due to his drug use. He was now unemployed. We thought any day the phone would ring, and he'd land another TV show or be cast in a movie or something. The phone didn't ring. He didn't work one day for the next two years.

Six months into our marriage, I discovered I was pregnant. I got a full-time job at a celebrity hair salon until our daughter was born. I was completely supporting us. That greatly whittled away at what little self-esteem Chip had left. He fell off the wagon several times during the next couple years, which only added to our stressed marriage. Chip escaped into alcohol and drugs because he was heartbroken that he was unable to provide for us. He could barely look me in the eye, and his old friends drugs, liquor, and nicotine, which I despised, gladly came back to keep him and us company.

Sloppy Agape

A Beatles' world-famous song includes the line, "All you need is love, Love is all you need." They're singing about human love, but don't be fooled, what we all need is God's unconditional love. God's love is not only perfect and unconditional but without judgment. The knowing and receiving of His great love is what heals, restores, and redeems us. The NT calls that, in Greek, *agape*. It is pronounced a-*gop*-py and sounds like sloppy. In the Greek and in Christianity, it gives "love" a new meaning. Agape describes the greatest degree of goodness and kindness, coupled with an unconquerable force of goodwill that always seeks the highest good of others, regardless of what someone else says or does to you. This love keeps no account of wrongs. It is a love that gives freely, without asking anything in return, and it does not judge the worth of its object. Agape is more a love by choice rather than feeling. Agape is the unconditional love God has for all the people in the world, every single one of us. His love never fails.

When I learned about the agape love, that we are loved with by God, I was convicted and decided that by His perfect and Holy Spirit in me, and by His amazing grace, I was going to try and love Chip and others in my life with God's agape love. Prior to that, I guess you could say I loved with a "sloppy agape."

I've heard it said, "God's love is His power, and His power is His love." I found that single statement to be revolutionary in my life. It drastically changed my understanding and heightened my desire to walk in God's love like never before. God's love toward us and God's love working through us is all-powerful. From now on, I would settle for nothing less from myself. In addition, if Jesus is the Lord of your life, we're all equipped, enabled, and empowered to walk and love with His perfect love. If God lives in you and me, we have no excuses, because God is love. My choice to love with God's love would sorely be tested.

Alexandria Noelle Mayer

In January of 1991, we joyfully welcomed our first child, a daughter, Alexandria Noelle Mayer. She was and is the perfect child I dreamt of and prayed for all my life. I'd always longed to be a mother and hoped to be the mother I never had. I was now more determined than ever to make our marriage work. Although my marriage had been enormously disappointing, I loved my husband, and I totally trusted God to heal him and…our marriage.

And God Said, "Pray to Me in Faith and I will…"

Soon after our daughter was born, we started receiving phone calls, letters, and visits to our humble little apartment from the IRS. We were both bewildered by this because Chip hadn't worked in a couple of years. These letters stated Chip owed an exorbitant amount of money, and it was accruing interest daily. We were OR I was gravely concerned about this outstanding debt.

During the years when Chip was working consistently and making a lot of money, he thought his manager and accountant had taken care of his taxes. We soon found out, that was not the case. He actually owed, with interest, a few hundred thousand dollars. The accountant wasn't necessarily at fault, but unbeknownst to Chip his taxes had gone unpaid for a few years.

I immediately began to devour the Word of God looking for His financial principles. One night I stayed up until 3a.m., searching the Bible and also listening to a well-known preacher speak on this very topic. When I finally went to bed that night, the Lord spoke to me and said this, "Pray to Me in faith and I will remove your debt." It was a unique experience because as the Lord was speaking to me, I was fully aware He was speaking. But I couldn't wake myself out of my sleeping state. It was the first time I ever heard the Lord's voice.

When I awoke the next morning and realized the Lord had spoken to me personally and given me a directive—complete with a promise—I wept nonstop for days.

I shared with Chip what the Lord had said, and we prayed in faith, just as the Lord commanded. We did that daily for several months and then we noticed, just as quickly as they began, the IRS phone calls, letters, and visits stopped. What a miracle my heavenly Father had performed on our behalf. I picture Him at a big, beautiful, gold desk, sitting in His office in heaven. And when He considered that we had obeyed and sufficiently prayed in faith, He simply pressed the delete button on Chip's debt. It wasn't reduced but completely removed as He'd said it would be, and it never resurfaced. Only a living God could do that. My heavenly Father, He's a doting daddy. With God, all things are possible.

Network Contract Offer

When Alex was about thirteen months old, we were still struggling financially. So I got an agent, too, and started pursuing acting jobs again. Right away, I landed a part as the love interest of a big male star on a primetime sitcom. The part called for a "Beautiful and Sexy" woman. The hair stylist and makeup artist worked their magic on me the Friday night we taped in front of a live audience at CBS, and I never looked so good. I didn't even look like myself. That's the beauty of TV.

The following Monday morning, I got a call from the studio asking me to come in and meet with the head casting director and a few other big shots on the studio lot where I had taped the show. They offered me a contract. Although we desperately needed the money, I knew I would have to leave my beloved daughter and husband every day to go to work, and I didn't think it was worth it. In truth, I was passionately in love with Jesus and serving Him, and wanted my life to bring Him glory. I realized my desire to act was completely self-serving, so I turned it down. I walked away from the offer and the industry and never looked back.

When we love and as we serve the Lord, there will be little and big tests along the way. I wouldn't necessarily have failed that test if I had decided to sign the contract with the network. But for who I was becoming at that time and how committed I was to the Lord, it was not the right decision for me. Money is not my God. I've never regretted that decision. God has always taken care of us. Whether it was through hard work or the generosity of friends or a supernatural blessing from the Lord, He has always heard our cry and met our needs. Praying to the Lord and waiting to see Him move in our lives, time after time. built our faith and was the very foundation for the Christians we were becoming. We learned to trust God in the hard places.

Our Saving Grace

After Chip was radically saved and liberated from his addictions, as a family we were committed to attending church. Chip had finally surrendered to the Lord. By the time we had our second daughter, Angelica Arielle (GiGi), in April 1993, he had gotten free. Our daughter GiGi practically came out of the womb laughing. She brought great joy to our family. Our daughters were then and are now the highlight of my life.

Chip was such a delight to be with and around, and he relished his role as a father. We were in constant prayer for our family, friends, neighbors, his family back east, mine in Texas, homeless people and talking about Jesus to anyone who would listen—this was the driving force in our lives. Our home was always full of friends and prayer. I called it the "Mayer House of Prayer." We read the Bible constantly, and Chip was finally on fire for God. I was so proud of him. He was rescued and set free by the power of Jesus, and I could hardly believe the godly man he was growing into.

Southern California—the Homeless Capital of the World

Chip became so caring for others that we couldn't pass a homeless person on the street without stopping and giving him or her money, frequently emptying his wallet. He would talk to them about Jesus and lead them to the Lord when he could. He'd give the jacket he was wearing if it was cold and they were without, or a beloved baseball hat. Sometimes he'd take the shirt off his back for a homeless person. If we saw someone standing on a corner, we'd drive through a fast food restaurant and buy them a meal and a drink or sometimes drive home, to cook them a hot meal, and bring it back to them.

We got to know one homeless man so well, Robert was his name. He was always at the same corner. Once when it was storming, we bought him a tarp and an umbrella and picked him up, and took him somewhere to get him out of the rain for the night. He had no teeth, and he also had multiple sclerosis. We grew to love him, he was a good man. We often went out of our way to check on him. I believed it was important for our daughters to witness us caring for others, realizing we are our brothers' keeper. One day Robert was gone, and we never saw him again. Chip led him to the Lord, so we believe Robert is in heaven with Jesus now.

Finally Chip started working as an actor again and did a few movies and TV shows. He was vibrantly happy and personally fulfilled for the first time in his adult life. We were the proud parents of two adorable little girls, and Chip and I were happy.

Youth Pastor and Women's Ministry Leader

Chip was asked to become the youth pastor (when he wasn't acting) at a small church that was also a school during the week. That was so rewarding for him. He was so much fun and gifted with children. He was like the Pied Piper.

I was homeschooling our daughters and had prayer meetings every Friday at noon in our home. I had also started ministering The Proverbs 31 Woman at The Church on the Way every week. I became an ordained minister in 1996. I loved the Word of God and was enthralled to minister and share His Word with others, especially women. I knew Jesus and His living Word could change their lives as it had mine. During the daylight hours, my Bible never left my side; it was always under my arm, so every spare second I had, I could read the Word. A couple of times I unintentionally took it with me to the grocery store. Each time I'd realize it was still under my arm, it made me laugh.

There was a time, before (Chip and) I got radically saved, I would have secretly admitted I was sad, shy, shallow, lost, and insecure. I was no longer any of those things. I was strong and confident in my God and who He was in me. My identity was now in Christ alone, and in Him, I lived, moved, and had my being.

In the year 2002 I established my own Christian non-profit ministry. I was being invited to speak at AGLOW meetings everywhere in Southern Cal and at mother's day teas, retreats, other churches and conferences, and Christian women's groups. It was so fulfilling and rewarding. Life was never more meaningful.

Both my daughters were born "sweet," as we say in Texas. God could not have given us sweeter or kinder children. They adored each other and played and giggled beautifully together. Alex and GiGi are unusually close, and I am grateful to God for their friendship and love for each other. They genuinely have each other's back. Homeschooling the two of them was one of the greatest pleasures of my life. I learned so much! We also cared a great deal and practically helped to raise Chip's first wife's daughter from her second marriage. She was and is such a little doll. She spent so much time in our home growing up that both of my daughters, to this day, think of her and speak of her as their sister.

Christian TV

I no longer had to be a private detective and house police in our home regarding Chip's drug and alcohol use. I hadn't in several years. While watching a CBN or a daily *700 Club* telecast, I heard them ask the viewers to write in their testimonies of God's goodness and deliverance saying this is how they got their stories that were taped and seen on air every day. I immediately thought of Chip and how much God had changed, healed and delivered him. So, I wrote to CBN about Chip's deliverance. The day they received my hand written letter, one of their producers called to interview us for the *700 Club*. They had already called us 3 times from Virginia before we got up that morning.

The producer flew to LA and interviewed us for a couple of days. They thought so highly of our interview that they saved it and aired it on *Harvest Day*. We were later told that our story brought in more salvations that year than any other taped interview. That meant a lot to us. Later that year, they flew us to CBN in Virginia, and we did a live interview with Terry Meusen. We were honored and humbled to bring glory to God for the great things He had done and continued to do in our lives.

The *700 Club* interviews aired often on TBN. We soon got a phone call to do our first TBN interview, and those frequent invitations continued for several years. We did numerous TBN programs, including the live program that aired at 7:00 p.m. We were thrilled to share our personal testimonies and to boast about our God and how He'd changed our lives so radically.

No More Policing

Over the years, the distrust, lack of respect, and policing I had to do in our home, looking for traces of his drug use, had damaged the intimacy in our marriage and our sex life. That created a lot of anger and resentment in Chip toward me. That was difficult to overcome, but we tried to get past it. I'm not sure he ever took responsibility for the role I was forced to play in our marriage, and I'm not sure he was ever able to fully forgive me for it, either.

The Evil Stepmother

After Chip stopped his substance abuse, our biggest problem, I am sad to say, was his daughter. My stepdaughter absolutely hated me from the very beginning and unfortunately, that never changed during the course of our marriage. We started dating when she was four years old. She was such a pretty little girl, extremely bright, and very precocious. Her parents divorced before she was two years old. Chip quickly remarried, and that ended in divorce almost right away, too. There was no stability in her precious young life. She deserved so much more.

She stole my things, lied about me, and lied to me. Through it all, I could see how confused and angry she was. Chip didn't know how to handle her, so he just indulged her. That was his style of parenting and easiest on him. Whether Chip was clean and sober or high and misbehaving, he was not raising his daughter with any wisdom. She was angry and undisciplined and had learned quite adeptly to manipulate to have her way. She was already in survival mode and didn't know it. It was her and her dad against the world and seemingly against me, too.

While we dated and after we married, she primarily lived with us. She created so much conflict between Chip and I that our marriage was almost doomed from the start. If there was any conflict or tension between she and I, regardless of what it was, he would side with her and would not correct or discipline her when it was needed. If I tried to parent her in any way, I was corrected, called out, and humiliated. It was the two of them **against me** and I was often left out of things they would do together. I tried to ignore or overlook the problems. I was great at living in denial, but was also trying to live, and love and forgive like Jesus and just didn't know how to balance it all. I was in a no-win situation.

My daughters were caught in the mix of all the dividing lines and lies. No matter what I did, I was the bad guy and made to look like the evil stepmother and that was a brand-new role for me. In Chip's eyes, she could do no wrong, and when it came to his daughter, I could do no right.

I had never been seen like that before. It was such a crafty assault, especially in light of the fact I was not guilty of being evil toward her. I just learned to deal with it and really tried to learn to love her unconditionally. Often I just tried to stay away from her. She hated me with a perfect hate, and it was difficult to live with her, to say the least. Again, My love walk was being tested, but that's how it's perfected.

So like a typical woman, I started buying and reading every book on blended families and step-parenting. I bought books on tough love and disciplining. I learned as much as I possibly could and tried to implement all the information I learned. I took classes at church and went to seminars on parenting. The problem was this, I wasn't the problem, Chip was. He wasn't interested in changing or disciplining his daughter, and somehow I remained the evil stepmother, and our marriage suffered greatly.

Our Sex Life Suffered

When a wife is disregarded and/or devalued by her husband over a long period, it takes its toll in the marriage bed. I reached a point where I did not want him to touch me sexually, but I did my wifely duty. He knew it was no longer a pleasure but an obligation for me, and he hated that.

I was hurt and deeply wounded by the way he treated me. That ongoing conflict became a nail in the coffin of our sex life and, over time, began to erode our marriage. He failed to recognize the way he sided with his daughter and disrespected me. We were never a team as parents should be. The rejection and disdain he treated me with was the most painful experience in our twenty-year relationship. Eventually, I learned to die to it for the sake of our marriage and our two daughters. I stayed and did the best I could to love and forgive him, because he failed to see his part in the problem. Above all, I did not want to divorce. I was picking up my cross and learning to die daily. And I was provided many opportunities to do so…daily.

Learning to Love Unconditionally

As the struggle inside our family and home continued and I was growing in the Lord, I began to see this was a spiritual battle. This painful experience was an opportunity to grow and learn to love. The soil of our marriage was rich with opportunities to learn to love and forgive. I needed to learn to love with God's perfect love. God's love, manifest toward one another, is what sets us apart and makes us, as Christians, different than the world. How else do we learn our lessons but in the fire? The Bible calls this the "furnace of affliction," which includes hate, rejection, and accusation. It means nothing to love those who love us. But when we love those who hate and reject us, that is the true test.

I was beginning to see the bigger picture. It didn't matter what Chip's daughter said or did to me. It only mattered to God how I responded and if it was done in love. That requires death to self to obey God so perfectly. I desperately wanted to pass that test for Christ's sake, and to have the peace of God in my heart and in our home. I knew God didn't send this problem my way, but He would sure use it for my growth and His glory. It was so difficult, and I'm sure I was far from perfect, but I was trying.

I began to do everything I could when she was around to show the love of God and not to respond to her hatred toward me. Jesus makes it very clear; if we call ourselves Christians, we are supposed to love our enemies, just like He did (Matthew 5:44).

Whether she or Chip noticed or acknowledged my loving behavior and disposition toward her mattered not to me. I knew God was watching. This I know: perfect forgiveness requires perfect love. My love wasn't perfected yet, but God's love is perfect, and if I couldn't love them both unconditionally, it was my fault and not God's. I was challenged by this. I relied on Him even more for His love to be poured out into and through me. I prayed and begged for it daily. I began to see the difference in myself. I thank God for His tests. They're painful, but that's how we grow (John 13:13–14). I'm not going to lie; it wasn't easy. But God gave me the strength and the grace I needed each day. Neither she nor Chip acknowledged the loving changes I was attempting to make, but that was okay. God saw and knew my heart.(Matthew 10:35–36, 38).

"I Died for You, Will You Die for Me?"

I was frequently reminded of something the Lord had asked of me early in our marriage. He had said, "I died for you, will you die for Me?" He repeated it over and over, all night long, much like a broken record. Once again, I was aware He was speaking to me but was unable to wake up. How humbled I was that He asked that of me. Again, I wept for days. I didn't take His question of me lightly. What did He mean by that, though? Was I in sin and didn't know it? Was I being corrected for it? I was not aware of any known sin in my life. I began to study the Scriptures to gain understanding, so I could die for Him, as He had asked. I knew He wasn't asking me to commit suicide, but it was unclear exactly what He was asking of me. Now, I think He was preparing me to know how to handle the rough road that lay ahead for me, especially in my marriage.

"Whatever it is, 'die to it,' don't focus on it, focus on Me and My love…"

My understanding of it today is this: He was asking me to become aware of the things in my life that were not of or from Him and to crucify my flesh nature and carnal desires. Anything that wasn't going to strengthen me spiritually, bring Him glory, or draw me closer to Him, He wanted me to die to. Paul said that he died daily in 1 Corinthians 15:31. As Christians, we are called to die to self so that we are freed to live fully for Christ and reflect Him.

The self, or flesh nature, is selfish, self-centered, and self-involved. The way to identify 'self' is to honestly examine what motivated a particular thought, word, or deed in question, or whether it was of God. If you can be honest with yourself, you'll discover very quickly who sits on the throne of your life. Whether it's you or God? I did.

"You're Dying as Fast as You Can"

Salvation happens in a moment, when we confess with our mouth and believe in our heart that Jesus is Lord and then receive Jesus as our Lord and Savior. But the sanctification process is being worked out in us every nanosecond of every day for the remainder of our lives. The dying process is the same. In fact, after I understood and embraced the dying process, I realized only then could I fully live for Christ. I wanted that more than anything.

I got up faithfully each morning at 4:30 a.m. and read and studied the Word and prayed for five or six hours or until the girls got up and we began homeschooling. I fasted more than I ate. I frequently had dreams, visions, visitations, and deep revelations and heard the voice of the Lord often. My relationship with the Lord was so real, so intense. I lived in a supernatural state.

Jesus proved to me over and over what a true and living God He is. It became my passion to share and prove to others that we serve a living God, and His name is Jesus. He is alive in you and me, as believers. What does that mean? It means His Holy Spirit comes to abide and reside in us individually; that's why we're called

His body. As believers in Jesus Christ, He comes to live His life and establish His kingdom through us now. What a great mystery this is. But it's true!

Once when I was deeply hurt by a dear friend, I was so wounded, that I realized I obviously wasn't "dead" yet. *Dead people don't hurt*, I thought. I was so disappointed in myself. I was diligently trying to die in every area of my life that I knew was my flesh and not spirit. I went to bed that night, feeling disappointed in myself and still deeply wounded. The Lord lovingly said to me that night in my sleep, "You are dying as fast as you can." Realizing the next morning that the Lord had comforted me and not condemned me, I was strengthened and encouraged. He had also given me understanding that the dying process is just that, a process. That was a meaningful revelation I'll never forget.

Chip, the Construction Worker

Chip began to make a stand for Christ in the parts he was taking as an actor. He would no longer take a part as an adulterous husband, lying boyfriend or an immoral character of any kind. If it didn't bring glory to God and his little girls couldn't watch Daddy on TV, he would turn down the interview or part. The calls from his agents came less and less frequently because of that, and his acting career almost died. The small church where he had been youth pastor went through some severe financial woes and was forced to close its doors. Chip was now doing full-time construction work again with our next-door neighbor to pay the bills. He was being painfully humbled. God was doing his pruning in Chip's life, and it was hard to watch. But it bore much fruit in his life at that time.

Liar, Liar

After a couple of years of working construction, and with few acting jobs coming in, Chip grew discouraged. Then out of the blue, he got a call from his agent to read for a part in a Jim Carrey movie. We were told Jim had actually asked to see Chip, by name, for this part.

Chip and I were faithful tithers and givers, but I thought the timing of this call was amazing. I had just sown a large financial (truly sacrificial!) seed in a ministry about seven or eight weeks prior. I named that seed a "revival in Chip's career." I watered that seed by praying over it daily. Trust me, I was praying in faith! He needed so badly to work as an actor and to feel good about himself as a provider. He read for the part in the film, *Liar, Liar* and got it.

He worked on that film for almost eight weeks. Every day he came home from the studio happier than I had ever seen him. Chip felt hopeful again in relation to his career. He said Jim was the funniest human being he had ever been around, and all they did on the set was laugh. It looked like things were finally turning around in his life, and his acting career was being reestablished. As God says in the book of Genesis on the days of creation, "It was very good."

Chip Was a Doting Daddy

Chip had become a solid Christian and was thoroughly committed to our family. He was a fun-loving daddy. He was the dream dad, the Disneyland dad. Being a child at heart, in many ways, he related more to the innocence of children than he did to adults. Our daughters looked at him like he was their hero. They practically idolized him. We loved taking them to the park and swinging them, and we spent much time in our backyard playing with the girls. They brought out the best in him. That summer he built a huge tree house for them in the backyard. It was spectacular. Playing back there and knowing Daddy had built it for them was a highlight in their young lives and a very special memory now. Just like our heavenly Father, Chip was truly an adoring, doting daddy in that season.

Alex, Shauna, Chip and GiGi
on their way to church

The New York City Soap Opera

After the movie *Liar, Liar* was released, and because of its enormous success, we expected lots of acting opportunities for Chip. But they didn't come. In the meantime, he kept doing construction work. He worked hard every day, but we were barely making ends meet. Deep discouragement was starting to creep in again.

Chip's agent called and said one of the daytime soaps in New York was interested in signing him to play a new character, and it would start soon. He explained Chip would need to sign a two-year contract and move back to New York. He was thrilled because he was raised back East. He'd be back home with all his brothers and sisters and their families.

It was an enormous amount of money, and he would be playing a preacher. Chip was elated, and we knew it was God giving this to Chip. We never questioned that he was going to nail it.

A total of five guys were up for the role, and they had to fly to New York and do a screen test with the girl who would play the character's love interest. They assured Chip he was the front runner. The soap negotiated the contract in advance, which is normal. He left for New York high as a kite and even called a Real

Estate Agent back East to look for a house for us. He was actually giddy with excitement. He left early one morning and flew back the following day. He was on pins and needles, waiting to hear their decision. His joy was short-lived.

No one told Chip the actress he'd be doing the taping with was only 4'11". Chip was almost 6'3" and had decided to wear cowboy boots for the taping. That put him at about 6'5". He was told the difference in their height didn't work on camera. They chose someone else for the part, someone much shorter.

To say Chip was devastated is an understatement. The enormity of this disappointment stole every ounce of joy he had and he was now severely depressed. But more than that, he took his eyes off Jesus and put them on himself and his disappointing circumstances. When he did, the spirit of self-pity stepped in, and he began to fall back into that dark place he'd been delivered from years ago. Chip wouldn't talk to us and didn't want to go to work. He quit going to church with us as a family. He became almost paralyzed with depression. I was deeply concerned and prayed around the clock as alarm bells were going off in every direction.

The Python at Our Door

A couple of months before the phone call came in about the soap opera, I had a terrifying dream. In the dream, we were living in our actual home. As I walked out our front door, I immediately saw a big, beautiful, colorful snake. This was no ordinary snake. It was a python. It was trying to hide, as it was coiled up and around the base of a big green bush, about four feet from our front door. It faced the door, its head erect. Its huge and almond-shaped eyes were more like a human's and were fixed and wide open—facing our front door. It was watching and waiting for something or someone. When I opened the door, its eyes did not blink, flinch, or look away.

Despite its piercing eyes, the python was captivating in its beauty. It was covered in large, exquisitely cut, sparkling, precious stones. I saw rubies, emeralds, sapphires, diamonds; there were stones of every color in the rainbow, and they were laid in gold. I could see them shimmering in the light. The python was alluring, attractive, and seductive. In Ezekiel 28:13, the Prophet describes Satan, or King Tyre, as having been in Eden, the garden of God, and every precious stone was its covering. I've seen it; I know it's true.

I froze as the python and I locked eyes. I then heard the Lord's voice quote this familiar verse to me from Genesis 4:7, **"If you do well, will you not be accepted? And if you do not do well, sin lies at the door, And its desire is for you, but you should rule over it."** With grave concern, I told Chip the next morning. We immediately began to pray against this assignment. The Lord was warning us through that Scripture there was an attack coming, but it should and could be "ruled over." I knew this was regarding my husband.

To say I was concerned about this warning is putting it mildly. This was the second time I'd seen this same python in a dream. The first time it was in our front yard, watching from a distance of about thirty-five feet from the door. Now it was at the door. The dreams were about ten months apart. I was baffled because Chip was no longer a threat with drugs or alcohol. He'd even quit smoking. *Thank God,* I thought, *that season is far behind us.* Life was so stable and steady now. Chip had been set free from his captivity, but I knew those same evil and familiar spirits still lurked around him, waiting and hoping for an opportunity to slither back into his life. That's how they work. The devil's tactics have remained the same as is spoken of in Luke 4:13, **"Now when the devil had ended every temptation, he departed from Him [Jesus] until an opportune time."**

I no longer questioned the existence of the evil force we call Satan and his demons. The kingdom of darkness opposes all that is good and is of God, but Jesus came to destroy the works of darkness. Jesus accomplished His mission over two thousand years ago at Calvary, when He was crucified at Golgotha for you and me.

Chip Said, "I'm Going Next Door"

Chip never went anywhere after work. He always wanted to be home with his family. One evening, soon after he came back from New York and discovered he didn't get that part, he said he was going next door for a beer. *A beer?* I thought that was unusual, but I hadn't felt the need to police him in years. I went to bed before he came home. Thinking nothing of it, I fell asleep.

I was abruptly woken up the next morning at dawn, to someone talking extremely loud in our home. I tried to figure out who it was and then I realized it sounded like Chip's voice, coming from the front part of the house. He sounded angry and was practically shouting. As I lay in bed, I grew scared. I quickly leapt out of bed to see what was going on. I ran down the hall and saw him standing in our dining area, close to the front door, naked, flailing his arms, and yelling at something invisible. He was speaking gibberish. He was sweating profusely; in fact, he was dripping wet, and the floor surrounding him was wet from his sweat. He must have been standing there, shouting and sweating for hours. Chip was completely out of his mind. I walked over to him to ask what he was doing. He didn't see me or respond to me at all.

I continued trying to get his attention. I yelled at him. I waved my arms. He never saw me. I was scared to death! I thought he had a mental breakdown due to his sorrow and sadness. I was alarmed and didn't know whether to call the police. I certainly didn't want our daughters to see their daddy like that. I called his 2 best friends and acting buddies and woke them up and begged them to come over. Sam Jones and Patrick St. Espirit both rushed over to help me. I knew they could handle Chip, put some clothes on him, and help me figure out what to do next.

I ran next door and asked our "trusted" friend and neighbor if Chip had been given any drugs the night before at his house or if he knew what might be wrong with him. He, of course, played dumb. He lied and denied knowing anything about what 'might' have happened to Chip the night before. I believed him. But then that left me further confused over Chip's mental state. Both of his friends quickly arrived, got his attention, and put some clothes on him. Chip began to come to his right mind.

We later found out the neighbor's friend brought over some meth and offered it to him. Chip didn't know what it was. He'd been clean for many years, but feeling devastated and defeated, he tried it. Chip made a choice that night. He chose not to rule over it. God didn't fail Chip. Instead, Chip failed to make the <u>right</u> choice. God was not to blame for Chip's weakness. Chip was in the pit of despair when that 'serpeant' slithered in and tempted him, and he didn't have the strength to resist. In 2 Corinthians 12:9, Jesus days, **"My grace is sufficient for you, for My strength is made perfect is weakness."** Chip was attempting to self-medicate in order to ease the pain of his recent disappointment. Unfortunately, he was craftily set up and greatly deceived, just like Adam and Eve. He's been a deceiver from the beginning...

That Was the Snake

That demonic spirit, represented by the python, watching and waiting for an opportunity, was the enticing temptation of drugs. Please know we are only tempted in areas where we're weak with desire. That's where and how the Devil traps us. **"Sin is** [and was] **crouching at your** [our] **door"** just as Genesis 4:7 read (NIV). In his saddened and weakened state, the drugs were appealing, seductive, and attractive to Chip, which were perfectly represented by the "beautiful" python.

Our marriage and Chip were never the same after that night. We had shared 7 good years together, while he was clean and sober and passionately loving and serving the Lord. From that point on, he wrestled with that drug and others like it the remainder of his life, which would be exactly ten years. That happened in 2001. As I recount that experience, I realize my own mind is filled with a type of fog regarding Chip and my marriage.

The Meth Addiction

Chip was now sad and ashamed. He began lying to me again about what he was doing and where he was going. He was also very angry. We had a double car garage to the immediate left and behind our home, almost in the backyard. A long cement driveway led up to it. Chip began to live out there most of the time. He worked out, listened to smooth jazz, and sat in the sun. Mostly, he was drinking while doing and hiding his drugs.

He wasn't working anymore, so while I was homeschooling our daughters and ministering at my church and many other places during the week, I was also our sole supporter.

His first wife and I had been working swap meets together for many years such as Rose Bowl, Fairfax and Orange County on the weekends. We sold clothes for women and girls. We took our clothes to studios, private homes, beauty salons, and boutiques. I also sold high-end purses and just about anything else I could get my hands on. I worked food shows in LA, Long Beach, and San Francisco. I cooked and sampled food at Costco, complete with a hairnet and plastic gloves. I sampled the expensive perfumes as a fragrance model at Saks and Neiman Marcus. I sold dancing shoes at Dance Competitions. I babysat my friends' children on our block. I worked conventions as a model for various large companies. I worked all the time, trying to support my children and I so, we weren't evicted from the home we had rented for so long. It was the only home our children had ever known. Our elderly, Christian landlord, Martha, was very kind to our family and never kicked us out, even if our rent was late. We loved and appreciated her very much. She was a gift from God to us.

Living in a Women's Shelter

Chip was becoming dangerous to live with, and I was growing more and more concerned about our safety. I did my best to hide his crazy erratic behavior from our girls. He'd quit the drugs for a short time, and just when I thought he might be clean again, he'd disappear on a binge. He'd come back unexpectedly and threaten me. I started to find his drug paraphernalia in the house and garage. I asked him to leave over and over, telling him it wasn't safe for the girls to be around him any longer. But he would not leave. He was high and paranoid and wouldn't and of course, couldn't work, nor did he want to. Needless to say, Chip was a completely different person when he was drunk or high.

I knew we had to move out. I started calling women's shelters, and none were available. I was in women's ministry and well aware of how difficult it is to find shelter for domestically abused women, especially those with children. I had made those calls for so many women over the years. Now I was making them for myself and my children. It was all too sad and surreal to believe. I couldn't find one for us, either.

I'd worn out the good nature and hospitality of most my friends since this meth nightmare began. My daughters and I slept on floors with people's dogs, in the car, and on friends' couches. We had to escape and run out of the house too many times in the middle of the night, when he woke me up high on drugs. I'd wake up the girls, and we always managed to escape. I usually didn't have much money and no credit cards, either.

I thought of my dear friend Trish Steele (one of the women in this book) and remembered she had a nearby shelter for women. I called her immediately. Believe it or not, a woman and her children were vacating their room that day, and we could come live at her shelter indefinitely—or as long as Chip didn't find out where we were. Those were my sentiments exactly. My daughters were terrorized and confused over their daddy's frightening behavior. And frankly, so was I.

I had such guilt over what I was dealing with in relation to my daughters and not having any options. I laid down my ministry for the summer. The church encouraged us to do that each summer. I kept ministering at other women's ministry meetings when asked. God helped meet our needs that way. We lived at the women's shelter several months.

Poverty, Extreme Poverty

Often during the years when Chip was doing drugs again, we were practically penniless. There were times we had so little money that I had to dig in couch cushions or the bottom of purses to find change to buy toilet paper. You know you're broke when you're buying toilet paper one roll at a time. I stood in many different free food lines in Los Angeles, and thank God, there are many.

Because of the hardships during those years, I grew spiritually in leaps and bounds as I pressed into God. I have learned God is totally trustworthy. I can say in all honesty, I am a blessed woman today because of all the things the Lord has brought me through. He is still a miracle-producing God, just like He was in the Old Testament and just as we witnessed Jesus to be in the New Testament. Regardless of the money we did or didn't have, "I have the true riches which cannot be taken away" an intimate relationship with my Lord and Savior, Jesus Christ.

Chip Got Clean Again

After the girls and I moved to the woman's shelter, Chip was now living alone in the house. He slowly began to straighten up again. He got clean and started calling and begging to speak with and see the girls. I didn't permit it at first. Then we would meet at a public park, and I would let the girls see him. He'd cry and apologize and beg for us to come home. Of course, he'd swear he'd never do drugs again. "He was miserable and couldn't live without us." He'd spoken to his boss and gotten his job back. Over a period of many months, I saw that he was clean and sober again, and gradually, I let my guard down, and we moved back home. What a roller coaster life had become. I was worn out.

One Night after a Miracle Crusade

One night, my worship leaders and I went to a miracle crusade in Anaheim. The girls were older, and both were spending the night with a close friend across the street. Chip was home alone while I was gone. He'd been clean and sober for several months.

When I walked into our house after midnight, wearing high heels and my favorite white ministry suit, Chip followed me down the hallway. He grabbed me from behind and threw me to the floor. He'd been doing meth while I was at the crusade. He had never been violent with me before, and it happened so quickly that I was scared for my life. Then he picked me up, threw me into our bedroom, and locked the door. He positioned himself between me and the door, so there was no possibility of escape. As I looked at him, I realized he was completely out of his mind on drugs. He began to speak to me with such hate and hostility that I feared he might kill me that night. It wasn't Chip. In disbelief, I cried and begged him to let me go, more concerned about what would happen to my daughters if he killed me. I wept while he continually told me to shut up. I decided to quietly submit to whatever he wanted. (There was that same evil, sexual assault – an ongoing assignment since I was 8 years old.) He angrily forced himself on me throughout the night and until morning. The sun finally came up, and he passed out. I unlocked the door and escaped the bedroom.

I quickly packed the girls things and mine and picked them up from across the street. We stayed with a friend and her husband, sleeping on the floor with their five dogs. We went through the same routine again, him getting clean and crying and apologizing, and eventually we moved back in with him. I wasn't crazy; I had no other options.

I Took Our Bedroom Door off the Hinges

Uncertain if I could trust him, when we moved back in, I took the bedroom door off of the hinges and hid it in our backyard, just in case he ever decided to hold me as a sexual hostage in the bedroom again. I no longer slept with him or in that bedroom. I slept with our daughters in their room.

Sure enough, months later, when I least expected it, he grabbed me and literally threw me in the bedroom after I came home from work one Sunday evening. And when he turned to lock the door, he was so baffled by not being able to find the door, that I was able to run out and escape. He chased me down the hall and ripped off my shirt and bra. He was trying to rape me while I was screaming. Then I asked where the girls were. I knew that would stop him in his tracks. As he turned to look out the back door, I bolted for the front door, quickly unlocked it, and ran out and down the street. With no top or bra on, I covered and cupped my breasts in my hands and I ran to a neighbor's house. I banged on the front door, screaming for help. They let me in and convinced me to call the police. It took me about an hour to make that decision, but I reluctantly called the police on him. At this point, I finally knew I had to protect myself. His continuous drug use and now violence toward me endangered my life and my daughters needed their mother.

By the time the police arrived, Chip had fled on foot. They took my daughters and me to the police station, and I filed sexual assault charges against him. I had a few cuts on my face from struggling with Chip. Afterward, we went to stay with another dear friend. My poor daughters didn't really know what was going on. I said very little. It was about three in the morning before we made it to my friend's house. The three of us slept on the floor that night with her new litter of kittens. Chip was arrested later that night, but due to his own stupid drunken, drug-induced behavior. Falling down in a public place, he drew attention to himself and the Police saw him and cuffed him and took him to jail.

Chip called me from jail to come bail him out. I didn't do that, instead I wrote the DA a note on Chip's behalf. I asked for leniency, so he would not be sent to county jail but to mandatory rehab, saying "He wasn't a bad man, but instead a sad and broken man, who desperately needed rehabilitation." I also said Chip was neither evil nor a criminal. Rehab could possibly save his life.

The DA read my petition. I had favor with him. A dear friend from my ministry board, who was an attorney, stepped in to represent him and plead his case. The judge ruled that if I could find him a bed in a rehabilitation program within two days, Chip could go to court-ordered rehab instead of jail.

Teen Challenge

Our friends and I furiously made calls, and sure enough, we found him a bed outside LA at a Teen Challenge. It was a mandatory year-long program. We went back before the judge, and I told him we had found Chip a bed. Chip was released from jail into my care, and I was responsible to deliver him to Teen Challenge by 7:00 p.m., or he'd go to jail. Chip had been in jail for three days and was detoxing, shaking, sweating, scared, and crying like a little boy. It had been heartbreaking to watch him sob in court. Now he was crying in my car and begging me not to take him to rehab. It was heart wrenching, to say the least. He was falling apart.

Chip entered rehab and eventually was glad to be there, considering his only other option was jail. He was gone, living at Teen Challenge, and receiving the help he so desperately needed. I had no intention of remaining in the marriage when he got out, but for now we were safe, and so was he. I was able to sleep soundly for the first time in years.

What Happened?

Hope deferred makes the heart sick.
(Proverbs 13:12)

Chip felt defeated and was hopeless.

That word "sick" used in the verse is the Hebrew word *chalah*. It means (*Strong's Concordance* #2470) to be weak, make sick, diseased, grieved, worn, put to pain, afflicted, to become weak or wounded.

All those things described or defined Chip. The disappointment of losing that soap opera job in New York, coupled with the introduction of meth on the heels of that loss, filled him with shame and stole his hope. He was hopeless, hurt, and angry. And the only way he knew how to cope was to hide his sorrow in drugs and alcohol—again. The Devil was watching and waiting.

The girls and I lived peacefully in our sweet little home and prayed for Chip every day. He called frequently and told us all how much he missed us and how well he was doing. He was clean and feeling strong again for the first time in a long time. Teen Challenge is a Christian rehab, so he was in the Word daily. That was positive. He felt confident he would come out clean and stay that way, finally.

Chip Was Forgiven

I had absolutely no unforgiveness toward Chip. But the sad truth was, I was deathly afraid of him now. I was having flashbacks of the threats and violence he had acted out towards me when he was high on meth. When he attacked and hurt me, sexually and otherwise, he hardly ever remembered any of it and always cried and repented to me incessantly. I knew he was ashamed and meant the apologies with all his heart. I knew it wasn't Chip but the drugs and the demons driving his behavior. Those demons wanted to kill him and me. It wasn't the real Chip. He had never hurt me when he was sober, ever! But at that point, I didn't think I could ever live with him again because of my fear of him.

Chip eventually got out of the rehab and on very good terms. He was clean and sober and very contrite but I was experiencing what soldiers and others sometimes have after experiencing traumatic events. I had post-traumatic stress disorder (PTSD). He came back home, and I lived in constant fear of him. I was terrified to be alone in the same room with him. I began to tremble if he got too close to me, and I planned my escape route, just in case.

He started working construction again, which he despised. The newness of his sobriety wore off, and he was desperately unhappy and depressed again. I had hoped and prayed that the therapy and counseling he received while in rehab would sober him up for good and heal him. We were two strangers living under the same roof. His acting career was dead and now he completely despaired of life.

The Marriage Ended

Within two years after Chip got out of rehab, our marriage finally ended. It was a very L O N G two years. I prayed our marriage could survive all his substance abuse and resulting physical abuse toward me, but I never got over my fear of him. He was a very angry man, now. I desperately wanted Chip healed and set free and wanted all to see, mostly his daughters, his healing and deliverance. I so badly wanted God to be glorified in Chip's life and for Chip to experience and to be seen as a trophy of His great grace. That didn't happen. He never stopped drinking and doing drugs. Chip seemed to absolutely hate me, too. According to him, everything was my fault. Come to think of it, that's exactly what Adam said about Eve. Remember?

A New Season

I had a lot of fear associated with being a single mom and had tried so desperately and for so long to avoid divorce. I never quit trusting God to do what only He could do. Toward the very end of our marriage, Chip and I were either ignoring each other or arguing, which I hated. One day with the *Dr. Phil Show* on in our living room, I overheard Dr. Phil say, "Better to be from a broken home than living in a broken home." That statement brought me to my knees. My kids were suffering greatly in our broken home. I believed the Lord was speaking directly to me that day through Dr. Phil for the sake of my precious girls. I knew it was time to begin to prepare for a new life. That was in 2005.

I slept on the couch the last two years of our marriage. One night, sleeping on my left side and facing the inside of the couch, the Lord woke me from a deep sleep. He stood behind and over me speaking His Word to me. He quoted Ecclesiastes 3:1-8, [1]**"To everything there is a season, a time for every purpose under heaven: [2]A time to be born, And a time to die; A time to plant, and a time to pluck up what was planted; [3]A time to kill and a** time to heal; A time to break down, And a time to build up; [4]A time to weep, And a time to laugh; A time to mourn, And a time to dance; [5]A time to cast away stones, And a time to gather stones; A time to embrace, And a time to refrain from embracing; [6]A time to gain, And a time to lose; A time to keep, And a time to throw away; [7]A time to tear, And a time to sew; A time to keep silence, And a time to speak; [8]A time to love, And a time to hate; A time of war, And a time of peace." Then He stopped. While He was speaking to me, I tried to turn over to see Him, but my body was completely locked as if I were paralyzed. I knew that night He was telling me that a season of my life was ending and a new season was beginning. The supernatural experience and impartation of His Word, which He personally spoke over me, was affirming and empowering.

Divorce

We hadn't moved out, yet, but things began to change very rapidly after the divine encounter with the Lord, that memorable night. A few months later, a very dear friend of mine and a member of my ministry board died unexpectedly. She left me a small inheritance which afforded my daughters and me the opportunity to move out and start a new life.

After a very ugly scene in our home at Christmas of 2005, I heard the voice of the Lord say to me, "This day you are released..." I knew He was talking about my marriage. I slipped off my wedding band, handed it to Chip, and calmly said, "I want a divorce," and asked him to move out as soon as possible. He refused.

I Gave Notice

Seven months later, on July 1 of 2006, I gave notice to our landlord that I (and the girls) would be moving out in 30 days. I did that with fear and trembling. My heavenly Father moved mountains for me in the next four weeks. By the end of the month, someone bought me a car, complete with the pink slip, and I was offered a full-time job with the largest Christian non-profit in the world—at the Divisional Headquarters of The Salvation Army in downtown L.A. (It is the greatest and most honorable organization I've ever known.) Then a pastor and his wife whom I had only met once called and offered their guesthouse for us to live in, close to the beach in Santa Monica. During the years of our marriage and hardships, God had given me the grace to stay. Now He was giving me the grace to go.

I enrolled my daughters in the local high school and thought they would love it. They were excited about that change but were much more wounded emotionally than I realized. It was a tough year. They were angry, and they cried often. I found out later they were deeply worried about their dad. I had a great deal of guilt associated with the divorce, but I knew it was the right choice for us all. I got them counseling to get through it. Though it was a difficult year, we lived through it. What didn't kill us, made us strong!

I came home from work every day, jogged to the beach and back home, crawled in bed, read the Bible, prayed and slept all weekend. I was so emotionally and personally exhausted and in need of healing. It was a much needed season of repair and because there was real peace, I was beginning to feel safe and rested for the first time in many years. I would walk around my little house, weeping with relief and praising Jesus! The house at the beach was such a blessing from my heavenly Father.

My daughters desperately missed their friends back in Sherman Oaks, where they had grown up. So after exactly one year at the beach, we moved back, and I enrolled them in a charter homeschooling program. They were much happier.

I missed the beach terribly. It was therapeutic for me. I missed my jogs and I missed the ocean. But my girls were so ecstatic and they were my priority. I wept the entire day we moved, but my girls were thrilled, and that's all that mattered to me. The sacrifice was worth it.

In the meantime, Chip's life had drastically fallen apart. He lost his apartment, and his car was repossessed. He started doing meth again and was no longer working, so he had no income. He lived with friends briefly, until he began to receive a SAG pension check. It was pretty substantial and he managed to stop the drug abuse, for a short time again. He got clean and moved down the street from us. The girls and I actually liked that he was close. We could look after him, and he sure needed it.

My Beloved Brother—Chip Mayer

It was two years since Chip and I divorced, and I saw him often with our girls. I drove him to do errands, since he had no car. It may be hard to believe, but I still loved him with all my heart. After he moved across the street, I often invited him over for dinner, holidays, birthdays, and so on. I occasionally let him spend the night in the girls' room. If he was sick, I took care of him. We had a sweet but sad relationship. He was my broken-down Christian brother now.

Despite his circumstances, Chip was still brilliantly witty and started making me laugh once again. We frequently reminisced and talked about the good times we had once shared. We reminisced and talked about the happy times we had shared. We usually cried together. I loved him so differently now. To the very end, I still had faith and hope that he would be healed and set free from his addictions once and for all. I never stopped praying for him. I was still afraid of him, but he was a complete gentleman and never gave me any reason to fear him again. The bad memories from the past still haunted me, though.

Believe it or not, he started proposing marriage to me every time I saw him. Although it was utterly ridiculous, he wasn't kidding. He knew I wasn't taking him seriously, but he hoped I would and frequently would do it in front of our daughters, too. They loved it. I often saw them turn their heads and try to hide the tears running down their cheeks, remembering when we had once been a happy family. We would all laugh about it together. Chip and I were such different people now. It was hard to believe we were ever married.

Without exception, Chip would sob and apologize for ruining our marriage each time I saw him. He knew I loved him, and I had forgiven him, but he just couldn't forgive himself. That's why he kept apologizing. He fully realized, retrospectively, that he alone destroyed our marriage and family. Chip also finally acknowledged the way he mistreated me in relation to his first daughter all those years. He felt ashamed about that, too. We cried together over our broken marriage often. I don't know if that's typical for most divorced couples, but it certainly was true for us. When he was clean and sober, he was such a sweet man, wonderful father, kind, and charitable. He was such an extraordinary person but just so self-destructive.

The Four Ambulance Trips in 2011

In 2011 Chip started drinking heavily again. I knew God was able to heal him, but Chip had grown too weak and weary to fight the good fight of faith anymore.

Our daughters were older now, with their own lives and friends. They saw less of him, and the less he saw of them, the more he drank. And the more he drank, the less they wanted to see him. He told us he was drinking because he was sad and lonely.

I walked across the street to check on him and visit with him frequently. Sometimes he'd call and ask me to pick him up some groceries or bottled water. I gladly obliged, and we'd sit together and talk and laugh about old times when I brought them to him. I enjoyed his company, in small doses.

In March, I walked over after work, and he didn't answer the door or his phone. He hadn't in a couple of days. I knocked and knocked, and he didn't answer. So I called the police. They had to break down the door. He was unconscious, lying on the wood floor with two big, bleeding, open wounds on the front and back of his head. He'd drank too much, fallen down, and a mirror had fallen on his head. The fireman and paramedics got him off the floor and into an ambulance. They rushed him to the nearest hospital ICU unit and saved his life. I chased the speeding ambulance down the LA freeways to the closest hospital. He had three brain bleeds from the fall. The ER doctor said I saved his life. I was so relieved and grateful to God that I found Chip in time.

My daughters and I visited him in the hospital daily. When he was released, I picked him up and took him home. He'd sobered up in the hospital, and we thought he would stay sober since he had almost died. He didn't. This same scenario happened three more times within the next eight weeks. Each time I picked him up as he was released from the hospital I made him repeat the salvation prayer (Romans 10:9–10) and made him repent of his sins. I had to be sure he was in right standing with Jesus and his salvation was secure, in case he died because of the reckless way he was living. We all feared the worst.

After work on Thursday, July 21, I walked across the street to see Chip. Now I had a house key for his safety. I knocked and he didn't answer, so I used my key to enter. I found him lying on the bed, in his dark bedroom, curled up in his comforter. He was so still, I feared he was dead. But he was alive and happy to see me. He started calling my name and stuttering. I thought that was odd because I'd never known him to stutter before. I had no idea that I was sharing the last few minutes of his life. His body and brain were shutting down.

He said he was hungry so, I ran to his kitchen but there was absolutely nothing in his refrigerator. So knowing what he liked, I went to the nearby grocery store and got some food and cold bottled water. I came back quickly and crawled into the bed with him. I spoon-fed him a container of cold, organic, low-fat, vanilla yogurt. It was his favorite thing in the world.

Then he said he was thirsty, so I held his head from the back and poured some bottled water into his mouth. It managed to go in. He then asked me for something else, which I had at my house, so I ran across the street to get that for him and ran back. When I arrived at his apartment, he was out of bed and dressed in a clean, crisp shirt and khaki shorts. He looked so nice. I was shocked because he had seemed so incapacitated earlier.

Chip was sitting on the couch, watching a Christian TV show. I sat in the chair beside him, and he started telling me how much he loved and appreciated me. He asked me to marry him, one last time, and we both laughed 'til we cried. He said, "Shauna, you know you're the love of my life, and I will never get over you or love another woman the way I love you." He thanked me for caring for him the way I did and apologized again for destroying our marriage. We hugged and cried. He cracked some jokes as I got up to leave.

I needed to hurry home because I'd invited a friend for dinner. As I left, he said, "Shauna, please check in on me this weekend. Neither my cell nor my landline are working. I didn't pay my bills, and they've both been turned off." I told him good-bye and reassured him I would check in on him. I left, leaving his front door wide open. It was Thursday evening, about five o'clock.

I went to work on Friday. After I got home, I felt such trepidation to go across the street to check on him that I decided not to go. I had a sickening feeling in my stomach. Both our daughters were busy all weekend, and for some reason, I was scared to go by myself. When Sunday came, I picked up my youngest daughter, GiGi, who's eighteen, and I said, "We must stop in and check on Daddy." When we pulled up in front of his building, she opened her car door and started to get out. I grabbed her and said, "We have to pray for what we may find when we go in there." She looked at me rather oddly, so I took her hand in mine and asked God to be with us, for strength, and so on. As I opened my door and got out of the car, my knees buckled, and I almost collapsed. I couldn't believe it. I really felt sick and scared for what we were walking into. Christ in me knew.

As we approached his door, I noticed it was still open, just like I had left it when I left Thursday evening. I walked in first, and there was Chip, sitting on the couch, in the same place I left him and in the same clothes. I thought he was sleeping. He wasn't. He was no longer alive. I was the last one to see him alive on Thursday. He must have passed as soon as I walked out of his apartment. How gracious of our heavenly Father. His body was still facing the door as it was when I left. The half drank beverage I'd brought from my house that day, was still sitting in front of him on the coffee table.

In 2011 Chippie Went to Heaven

Chip looked so peaceful. He was finally at rest. I like to imagine Jesus coming into his living room and carrying him with Him up to heaven. Once again, but now crying uncontrollably and in disbelief, I was calling the police, one final time. Was this really happening? Within minutes, his three daughters arrived, their boyfriends and friends, his first ex-wife, lots of our old friends, neighbors, police, paramedics, firemen—all in his small living room with him. It was a room full of sobbing women. It was determined he died of natural causes. His heart had finally had enough and gave out.

None of us will ever be the same without Chip here. He never realized how much he was loved and adored by us all. We were all devastated as we watched him slowly kill himself through drugs and alcohol over the years. No matter what we did, we were powerless to change him. Only God could do that. God is more than able to do that, too, but Chip couldn't seem to separate himself from his demons. For so long I thought if I just loved him enough, he would be healed and delivered. But it takes God's love and power to make that change, and a decision on the part of the addict to stop that behavior and never look back. Remember Lot's wife? She was warned not to look back at the pleasures of her sin and her past, as she left Sodom, or she'd be destroyed. She disobeyed, turned to a pillar of salt, and lost her life. That's a warning for us all (Genesis 19:17–26).

Chip and I had our differences, especially towards the end of our marriage, but I dearly loved him. I cared about his well-being and only wanted the best for him. I am eternally grateful for our beloved daughters and the years of wonderful memories we shared.

Since his passing, I see things a bit differently. I see how God alone strengthened me through the many turbulent storms of life. He taught me how to be a loyal and devoted wife, regardless of the circumstances. I honored my vows, especially when Chip needed me most. It would have been so much easier just to leave, but I wanted God to have every opportunity to change and heal Chip so, I stayed, prayed, and fought the good fight of faith. I do not regret my choice for one second. I am shocked by how his death has impacted me. The heavy weight and feeling of sadness and loss are almost overwhelming. I have a new depth of compassion for others who are experiencing the death of a loved one. On this side of eternity it seems so final. Believe it or not, we all miss him terribly. His personality was larger than life in many ways.

Chip's Not Dead

Chip's not dead! He's never been more alive! He has eternal life in and with Christ Jesus and has been liberated and set free from every bondage. He has a glorious body in heaven and is with Jesus and in the presence of the Father right now. I assure you, he's not missing Hollywood Boulevard; he's celebrating on Hallelujah Boulevard and walking on streets of gold. We don't grieve for our Christian family members and loved ones like the world does, because we know we will be reunited with them in heaven. Death has been swallowed up in victory. We never die, although our bodies do. We live our life here, in Christ, with the hope of heaven. Do you have that assurance of heaven? Are you sure? You can be.

Love with all Your Heart

Chip's passing has given me a new prospective on life and love— love without judgment, love freely, love everybody, forgive quickly, like Jesus. We need to love people with the love of God, because ours is so insufficient. Despite Chip's addictions, he was filled with love and hypersensitive and incapable of dealing with hardship. That was really his issue. He lived to help and serve others and did it without expecting anything in return. He loved being a blessing. He loved children, and they loved him. When he was sober and loving Jesus, he was becoming Christ-like.

People judged him because of his addictions. But no one hated them more than Chip did. It was the monkey on his back that he just couldn't seem to shake off. His own sadness, despair, and self-pity kept pulling him back again and again to that same dark place. If he couldn't shake the addictions in his life, try as he did, please know drugs are not something to play around with … ever. In my humble opinion, there's no such thing as recreational drugs. They open the door for demonic strongholds and the kingdom of darkness and that only comes to steal, kill, and destroy.

My focus now is to help save people and get them healed and set free from all demonic enslavement and bondages that hold people captive. I take that fight seriously, and I do that with the name of Jesus, the Word of God, the blood of the Lamb, by faith in God, and by the power of His Holy Spirit. You can too! As Christians, those are the weapons of our warfare.

Jesus Christ saves us, but the Holy Spirit changes us. We must look to, lean on, and depend on God and His indwelling Holy Spirit to lead and guide us to victory. God is faithful to heal, deliver, and redeem. But we must do our part and stand and fight the good fight of faith. God is able. In fact, He is more than able! Look to Him.

Demons of Drug Addiction

The demons of addiction deceived and tormented Chip. I witnessed personally, the cunning deception, destruction and ultimately, the untimely death the devil desires for us all. Watching it unfold has made my fight against the powers of darkness that much more ferocious. For many years Chip was a major threat to Satan's Kingdom. He never fully realized that, because the attack was so great against him that he couldn't see how mightily he was being used by God. Chip was a powerful preacher. I saw grown men cry openly at an event he preached at years ago at CBS Studios. They cried unashamedly and were convicted when they heard Chip minister the "living and life-giving" Word of God.

His Home-going Service

As a minister of the gospel of Jesus Christ, I have presided over many funerals. But I never anticipated presiding over Chip's. God helped me put together a memorable and meaningful service. I did that so his daughters could say good-bye and have a degree of closure. If I had not have done that for Chip, there would have been no service at all. Of course, his eldest daughter was there, and I'm happy to say we made peace several years ago. There were a few hundred friends, family members from back east, and loved ones. The "General Lee" from *The Dukes of Hazard* was driven out front of the church, and good friend Byron Cherry, who played Coy, was present and of course all of us X-wives.

My hearts-cry to you today is this: be compassionate and patient with your loved ones. Don't walk away when they need you the most. Remember, love is not just a feeling but often must be an action you make for Christ's sake and others. **"Love suffers long and is kind,"** 1 Corinthians 13:4 says. It goes on to say in verse 7, **"[love] bears all things, believes all things, hopes all things and endures all things."** When tempted to do otherwise, always choose love. Don't judge. That's God's job, not yours.

If someone you know has a drug or alcohol problem, please don't take it lightly. Unless you are a professional in that field, try to get them help, and never stop praying. Pray in faith, knowing God is able to heal and deliver your loved one. Be diligent, vigilant, and militant as you take your stand against the evil one. Remember, addicts aren't necessarily bad people, they're just broken and usually in pain. They need to know they're loved.

Mother Teresa of Calcutta once said, "If you judge people you have no time to love them." We're all so flawed, who are we to judge, anyway?

Chip Was a Blessing

You may not understand this, but in spite of himself, Chip was a blessing in my life. I assure you, I'm not referring to any form of abuse, but while fasting, praying, and waiting to see him healed and set free, I got radically saved myself. I am truly blessed because I got to know the God of the universe and Jesus Christ as my personal Lord and Savior throughout this spiritual battle for my husband. As I diligently sought God for almost twenty years, hoping to see Chip delivered, God revealed Himself to me time and again and proved to be a doting daddy and a living God. I saw miracle after miracle unfold in our lives during my relationship with and marriage to Chip. So many miracles, I can't begin to share all the unbelievable, incredible, and supernatural things the Lord did in our lives. There were literally hundreds of incidents where His amazing grace and unmerited favor were evident and resident. Get to know Him and see for yourself. He's real and He's waiting to reveal Himself to you!

When we get to heaven, I think we are going to have such a different prospective on our lives. The things we thought were a curse, we'll see were ultimately a blessing if it caused us to develop a deeper relationship with Jesus and taught us to trust in Him more. Ironically, the things we may have considered blessings here were meaningless or ultimately took us farther away from God; they were nothing more than distractions or what the Bible calls lying vanities.

Plus, I have Chip to thank for the two most wonderful gifts God has given me, our daughters Alex and GiGi. They are incredibly special, loving young women. They have seen a lot, and both have powerful testimonies already.

*GiGi and Shauna and Alex playing
around one afternoon.*

To love and be loved. That's what this life is all about. Right? Isn't that true for you? It is for me. Nothing else really matters. That's why Jesus came—to love us and show us how to love each other. Yes, He came first to redeem us and restore us to a relationship with our heavenly Father. Without the power of His Holy Spirit working in and through us, we can't love others or live our lives in a way that glorifies God or has any eternal value. Our faith works through love.

God gets all the glory for any good thing I may have done, endured or accomplished because He enabled me. In fact, any good thing you may have just read about, please know I am nothing and can do nothing without Jesus Christ and His strength and love empowering me to do so. I can safely say He's been my enabler!

All You Need Is Love

If you get nothing else out of my life story, please hear this—make love your goal in all you do, at all times and at all costs. God has given us His perfect and Holy Spirit to equip, enable, and empower us to live and to love perfectly and unconditionally, just like Jesus showed us. We strive for perfection, knowing we'll never achieve it in this life, but maybe we can achieve excellence. If you're not living your life that way now, it's not God's fault. It's yours, regardless of your personal circumstances.

Jesus said in John 13:34, **"A new commandment I give to you, that you love one another, as I have loved you, that you also love one another."** Verse 35 reads, **"By this all will know that you are my disciples, if you have love for one another."** Did you get that? Jesus said it's a commandment, not a suggestion.

Let that be your life's goal as well as God's commandment to you and your commitment to Him. Love God and others with all your heart. I promise you this is a commitment you will never regret, and great will be your reward! Christ within you will help you love others as He loves you. Let's all get busy giving away God's love. Freely you have received, now freely give. Did you get that? It's free!

Sinners Welcome

If you haven't committed your life to Jesus, STOP and do it right now! The good news is sinners are welcome into God's family and kingdom because there are no other kinds of people. But make no mistake about it, the sinners who are welcome in God's kingdom are those saved by grace through faith in Jesus Christ. It is the gift of God (Ephesians 2:8). Getting "saved" is as simple as the ABCs. Open your mouth and pray to the Father, in Jesus' name - the following three things;

A. *I acknowledge* to you, God, that I am a sinner and that I need forgiveness for my sins.

B. *I believe* Jesus is the only Son of God, and I ask you now, Lord Jesus, to come into my heart and save me.

C. *I confess* with my mouth that Jesus is now my personal Lord and Savior, and I commit my life to Him forevermore. Amen. Hallelujah!

You have just been born again. Welcome into the family of God and the kingdom of heaven. That is the sinners' prayer that you just prayed and confessed, which you'll find in Romans 10:9–10.

Together, as His beloved bride let's;

Spread His Word,
Shine His Light,
Share the gospel of Jesus Christ!
Let's get started sisters, we've got no time to waste!

Shauna Mayer Ministries
P. O. Box 55876
Sherman Oaks, CA 91413
818 8551404 (office)
818 3241456 (secondary number)
Website: ShaunaMayerMinistries.org
E-mail: Shauna@ShaunaMayerMinistries.org

Trish Steele

And do not be conformed to this world, but be transformed by the renewing of your mind, that you may prove what is that good and acceptable and perfect will of God. Romans 12:2

In the Beginning

My mother was only fifteen, young, beautiful, and looking for love to fulfill her emptiness. She went to a dance hall in Los Angeles and met the man of her dreams, Harry A. Blanco. He had passionate eyes for my mother, Lorraine. It was the beginning; two souls met for the first time and immediately fell in love. They met again shortly thereafter, and fell into an intermittent relationship. Little did my mother know she was pregnant with his baby. Her life was about to change dramatically. Harry and my mother eloped as soon as they could.

My father was a man with values and integrity at an early age of twenty. He was a carpenter, serving in the navy. He was so proud to have his first daughter, Patricia Jean Blanco. His full-time job and the requirements of the navy base in Long Beach did not take away from the wonderful times he spent with his family.

Our family was growing and happy. My mother became pregnant two more times and had three children by the age of nineteen: Patty, Debby, and Butch. How beautiful that my mother was able to have three children with a man she loved, and he actually took responsibility for his family. By today's standards, this was a rare relationship because so few young people want to take responsibility for their actions. I do not recommend any teenager try to start a family or have sexual intercourse outside marriage, because great hardship usually follows.

The first five years of my life with my father and mother were wonderful. My parents thought it would last forever. Unfortunately, our happy family had to deal with a tragedy shortly after I turned five.

Under the Curse

Our family was traveling to a camping trip with my father's Boy Scout group. I was thrilled to be with everyone at the campgrounds near the scenic lake. My father was a real man's man, with great passion and energy for family gatherings. My mother was fortunate to have a husband who gave us so much attention and love. And we were so lucky to have such a father.

When evening arrived, the four men (including my father) decided to go on the lake in canoes. They had the crazy idea of playing tug-of-war in the middle of the lake, with no lights, only darkness surrounding them. My father's canoe tipped over, and he and his partner were unable to turn the canoe back over. My father decided to swim back to shore. An hour later, the other men noticed he never made it back to shore. Park Rangers were called to search for his body.

As I looked out the window the next morning, I saw a group of people in tears, looking down at a covered body. I was told not to leave the cabin. My heart raced, and I began to feel frightened about my father. No one would tell me anything. I was only five years old, and the adults felt it was not appropriate for me to know just yet that my father drowned. I clearly remember the tears that rolled down my face as I sat in the car, knowing my father was dead and gone forever.

Why did this happen to my father? He was a good man and a loving father with great values. How can God take a good person away? Have you ever asked this question about a loved one? It took me years to find some answers. It seemed our family was under a curse.

My mother was only twenty-one with three children, no high school diploma, no work skills, and no referrals or resources to help her. What now? How would we survive? Could a mother meet the needs of three children, a mortgage payment, and put food on the table? (My heart goes out to single mothers who have no financial support.) My mother was unable to meet our needs. She was losing her mind and having a hard time living with memories of our lovely home, which my father provided. She was forced to sell the house and move home with her parents with her three young children.

Months after my father's death, my mother discovered I had a severe hearing loss and needed special care. I was put in a "deaf and dumb" school at the age of six. Today, they would call this school "hearing impaired," but in the '50s, everything was much different. And I was very different, too! I was one of the first students to learn to read lips. Most of the children did not like me, because I could talk and did not know sign language. I was rejected and bullied in the school. The sadness of my father being gone and being bullied took a toll on me. I begged my mother to let me leave that school. Two years later, she finally enrolled me in the neighborhood school. I was becoming adept at reading lips. Now I was able to step out and practice reading lips. For the first time, I felt special. I got extra attention from the teachers, and I noticed many people took time to look at me with smiles. I was the new, pretty girl in the school.

My grandmother had told me many times, "You are special." Her Catholic beliefs and faith always made me feel good when I saw her praying. Those words gave me hope and helped me to get through the tough times. God provided someone to pray for me. I know without my grandmother's prayers, I would never have made it through life.

Being Deceived

Three years later, my mother met a man at the navy base in Long Beach. She fell in love, and in less than a year, they were married. In the beginning, our stepfather was kind and took us places. But a few months into the marriage, he became a different person. He laid down some strict rules. We were forced to eat foods we hated. The food was sometimes shoved down our throats. We received harsh slaps across our face if we said anything he didn't like. Our stepfather treated us as if we were in a military boot camp, preparing for a horrifying battle ahead. There were many tears ahead for the three of us and years of abuse, beatings, intense fear, and vomiting food we hated. Our stepfather was a nightmare, and our mother didn't do anything about it. She was too insecure and hopeless about her ability to raise her children. She'd been deceived by the Enemy, and he seemed to want to destroy us all.

My stepfather began to play a "tickle game," which led to touching the innocent parts of my body and then to molestation. Now I was really afraid of him, because he would say to me, "If you tell your mother about this, she will leave you and never come back for you." That lie convinced me my mother loved him more than she did her children.

After one year of steady abuse, I couldn't bear it any longer. "You will never be anyone, you're too stupid!" my stepfather said. Those words rang in my mind. *I am going to prove him wrong!* I said to myself. My hearing loss left me with a speech impediment. I decided neither of these setbacks would hinder me from accomplishing great things in my life. I would not let this dirty little secret about my stepfather keep me in bondage to fear.

I finally found the courage to tell my mother what my stepfather was doing to me behind closed doors. She was shocked but remained calm. After four years of planning, saving, and seeking counsel, she got a divorce and was able keep the house. Now she was taking responsibility and started plans to go back to school to get her GED.

But the damage our stepfather did to all of us physically and emotionally left many deep scars. Some scars are still being treated after forty years with my brother and sister. But Jesus is the Healer, and our past can be healed and restored.

Have Mercy, Oh God!

My teenage years were full of chaos. People were not sensitive to the feelings of teens with physical handicaps. I did not want to be labeled "deaf and dumb," a common phrase used then. I did not want to be known as one who could not talk right. I did not want to be told I would never amount to anything. Who does? I was on a mission to seek acceptance, but in all the wrong places. I became a good liar about my speech and hearing impairment. I had everyone around me believing I was a foreigner with a cute accent. If I did not hear or understand what someone said, I acted as if I was not interested and acted like a snob. I had to play the game to be accepted in high school.

All the trauma I went through since the age of five was devastating to my health. I developed bleeding ulcers at the age of seventeen. When I became sick with hepatitis, I knew I could no longer take drugs to numb the pain from the past. Every teenager needs mercy. It's such a difficult time to reconcile the mind with the emerging woman's body and emotions.

"Where are you, Daddy?" I would ask as I cried alone in my bed at night, hoping to find an answer to all my problems. I wanted my real father back. He loved and cared for me, and I was his pride and joy. How could he be taken from me? Did I deserve this painful life? If my father were here, this would have never happened to me. "God, have mercy. Do you even know that I exist and that I need you?" I needed Him desperately and cried out to Him often.

Beauty from the Inside Out

In my last two years of high school, I was able to develop a wonderful relationship with the family next door. There were nine children, and one of them was my age. Her name was Kiese. She was bright, cool, and understanding. We became best friends and did a lot together. She was the only person who did not ridicule me because of my hearing loss and speech impairment. Instead, she was a good influence in my life, and through her friendship, I was able to overcome my fears of failing in school. She was a godsend! In our senior year, she encouraged me to enter a local beauty pageant. I thought, *I have the looks, and I can dance. But my speech is a mess. Is it possible for me to go onstage without making a fool of myself? I need help, and Kiese is the perfect person to bring the best out of me.* Today, forty years later, Kiese is still my dear friend.

The competition was on, and I was willing to learn how to bring out my inner beauty and gifts. The inner beauty is our soul, and my soul needed healing. I had to share all my insecurities and my painful past with Kiese. My friend did not realize she had a natural gift of counsel. Kiese later became a nurse to counsel youth sent to juvenile hall.

My confidence developed as I practiced daily in the mirror and began to see myself as someone with great potential. The night of the pageant, Kiese helped me through all my scenes, from my interview to my talent as a dancer to 007's "Goldfinger." She had to paint my body from head to toe with gold paint. My performance went perfectly! The pageant gave me confidence and a new outlook on life. I came in fifth place and was happy with my performance. People signed my yearbook, "To the Golden Girl," and that is just what I needed to believe I was special.

A Wrong Marriage

After graduating from high school, I was determined to find a new way of life. I went to Hollywood and explored opportunities in the model and media industry. I was able to make a decent living as a waitress, model, and makeup artist, juggling jobs while finding answers for myself. I was in great shape, dancing at night and meeting people I enjoyed. Finally feeling confident, I met a man in the nightclub who liked me and promised me the world. I fell for him, and being naïve, I thought this was *the* man for me.

Six months later, he and I moved to Las Vegas. I met a producer there, who wanted to use me for his film, even with my speech impairment. He must have thought I was a foreigner. Well that did not happen, because my boyfriend was worried about the attention I was receiving from this movie producer. "Let's get married and move back to California, and we'll buy a home and start a family," he said to me. This seemed like the best thing to do, not knowing I was already two months pregnant.

I accepted his informal proposal, and we moved to a beautiful home in Diamond Bar, California. It all felt so right. I was pregnant just before we moved into our new home, eager to start our new family. Seven months into the pregnancy, my marriage was falling apart. He was unfaithful, staying out many nights of the week.

I was sad and depressed. I no longer wanted to stay in the same house with my husband. But I needed to have my baby before I left him. It is known now that the fetus feels emotions, like acceptance and rejection, while still in your womb. After years of counseling women through my ministry, I have discovered many women who probably experienced these emotions in the womb and it greatly affected them.

I needed to make the right decision. I knew being a single mother would be hard, and life without some type of steady job would be a struggle. Who could I trust to take care of my child while I worked? I thought about the hardship my mother endured, trapped in a bad marriage and having to find means to support us after the divorce from my stepfather. I had to find alternatives for my child to have a good life, rather than repeat what I went through. Have mercy on us, God!

After my beautiful little girl, Shawna, was born, I had to find a new place to live. My husband and I sold the house and went our separate ways. He was not in the position to be a father to his daughter, as his playboy lifestyle was unpredictable. It was my job to raise her and make the best of it. I was very fortunate to have wonderful in-laws who loved their grandchild and offered to help raise her while I found a new career and began a new life for us. My in-laws were very successful and had the money to see that Shawna had the best education, and they loved and adored her. But Shawna needed her mother, too. What a mess I had made, choosing to marry someone for security instead of love.

Have Mercy on Me

I knew my marriage was over but did not file for divorce immediately. I had to focus on my life and career. Being a cocktail waitress was not a career. I was good at sewing, makeup, and fitness. I concentrated on art in high school but never pursued it in college or any trade school until an opportunity presented itself. I found a job at a Jack LaLanne Health Spa within weeks after moving into my new apartment. It was a good career opportunity. I was asked to do a modeling ad for the spa. I had done some modeling in the past and loved posing in front of the camera. It allowed me to feel beautiful and happy. This was a stepping-stone to the new career that was about to turn my life around. "I am going to be somebody one day. I'll show him!" I said to myself. My stepfather's words still haunted me as I tried very hard to be "someone."

I had gotten my body back quickly after my pregnancy. I decided to get an agent and model on my days off. It was one of my dreams to become a model and use my makeup skills for the entertainment industry. "Hollywood, here I come," I said as I drove down Hollywood Boulevard to meet with a photographer. The photos came out great. Now it was time to get an agent. I was driven to prove myself in this career.

About a year later, my boss at Jack LaLanne's, Nancy Baker, had some bad news for me. She was giving up the business. Nancy was the first woman I had met who was a Christian. Nancy's daughters, who worked part time at the spa, would talk about their church in Orange County. They made it sound like it was the most exciting place! I never thought of church being exciting. I had only been to a Catholic church, where the priest spoke in another language.

But something touched my heart when I was around Nancy and her daughters. They had a true innocence in them that radiated such love and purity. I wished my life could radiate that. *If my life hadn't been so difficult, being molested and abused, Christians might have accepted me into their lives,* I thought.

Nancy sold the spa and moved to Hawaii. I was going to miss her and her wonderful daughters, who showed me the love of Christ. I didn't realize then that Christians were supposed to radiate the love of Jesus to others. This left such an impression with me. Only years later did I realize how God used this experience to touch me and draw me to Him.

Feeling Empty

My life became very self-centered. I had many dreams and goals I wanted to accomplish, but no time for my little Shawna. She was placed in the hands of my former in-laws for five years. During that time, I signed with a modeling agency, received certification as an esthetician and makeup artist from beauty school. I had many opportunities to travel and meet important people in the entertainment industry. I was living a fast-paced life, modeling, doing beauty pageants, and making good money. Hollywood was being good to me, and I felt successful. But the feeling was fleeting because something was missing in my life. I wondered, *what is this void I am feeling?* I couldn't find enough things or activities to fill that void. *Why is my life so empty after achieving my goals and having almost everything a girl would want?* I couldn't figure it out.

At this point, another man came into my life. He was a successful businessman and had a daughter from his previous marriage. *Maybe my soul mate,* I thought, *and someone with whom my daughter and I can share our lives with.* I thought maybe this would fill the void that I couldn't seem to shake. *I must get back to being a mother and take care of my daughter—and his daughter, too. We can be a happy family, like the family I never had.* I went back to my former in-laws and got my daughter, and we moved into his beautiful home in Marina Del Rey. She was so happy to have her mother full time, even though her grandparents did a wonderful job raising her for years.

My life became consumed with this man. He did not want me to work for anyone or have friends or business associates. We had everything we needed, and he wanted to travel and keep me busy with only him. At first this was exciting and adventurous. But I missed my friends, especially those who had helped me in my career. I wondered, *why is he being so possessive with me?*

About two years into the relationship, the emotional abuse began. This time I was trapped and couldn't find a way out. This man had convinced me he was the best thing that could ever happen to my daughter and me. He spent thousands of dollars to keep me in the relationship, including paying for my divorce. He hired a maid and furnished his house with new items to entice me to move in. He made me believe nobody loved me the way he did. Was this love or obsession?

The abuse cycle was occurring in my life again, and I was reliving the life I had as a teenager. I never thought I would experience it again. I began to feel hopeless again, and once again, I needed to get my daughter and I out of this situation. *Now I fully understand the hardships my mom went through with my stepfather,* I thought. I began to plan an escape from the house with all my belongings and without him knowing. It seemed impossible, because I worked for him, and he kept me with him most of the time. We seldom associated with friends and definitely not mine. Besides, who would believe he was abusing me? He had a good reputation, and everyone admired him for his great business success. This sounds like my stepfather's scenario. I am saddened about the mess I put myself in again. Unfortunately, many women fall into this trap. We need a Savior to heal us from our wounds. Only then can we move onto a life filled with peace.

One night we visited a friend's house. We were all sitting in the Jacuzzi, talking and drinking a lot of wine when my fiancé or should I say abuser, asked me to do something that was unbearable. I refused. He became angry and took a swing at my face. I immediately put my hands up to protect myself. He hit the wineglass in my hand, and it shattered into my face. I ran into the bathroom and saw blood all over me. *This is worse than dying,* I thought, *because now I will have to live the rest of my life with scars on my face.* The other couple witnessed what happened and they were shocked. "I must go now," I said to the couple. This was the perfect time for me to escape from this relationship.

I left the friend's house feeling violated and enraged that I'd allowed things to go this far. There had seen so many red flags. The friends wanted to help, but I knew I needed to go to the police. I drove straight to the police station to report what he'd done. Hours later, they picked him up and put him in jail for domestic violence. Next, I had to check myself in to the emergency hospital to get some help, because my face was still bleeding above my brow line.

"May I help you?" asked the nurse.

"Yes, I have been battered by my fiancé and need to have someone look at the cut on my forehead." It was pretty deep. I had no insurance to give to the nurse, but she was so kind and understanding of my situation.

As I walked into the emergency room, a doctor was there to greet me. "Tell me what happened." I told him the whole story. As I was talked, I sensed everything was going to be okay. The doctor said, "Don't worry about your forehead. I can fix it so you will never know you were hit by that man's hands." My life has never been the same since that doctor got hold of me. His compassionate word spoke life into me. He had plastic surgeon skills and did a wonderful job stitching me up. I never received a bill from the doctor for the work he did. The stitching left no scar on my face. He was a doctor sent from God. What a miracle! For the first time I realize God really did care about me, and He was now drawing me to Himself.

Love is the greatest gift of all! I needed to find out where I could find and feel this love and compassion in other people. There is hope, and I was going to find the way to a new life.

Searching for God

In April 1984, I was desperately searching for something, a new mission in life. I found myself back at the health spa, getting in shape. As I exercised, a nice-looking man walked in and sat on the cycle next to me. There was something different about this man. He began a conversation with me, and in a short time, I asked him, "So Thursday nights you attend a Bible study. Can I go?"

"Sure you can go. It would be my good pleasure to take you," he said.

"Where is this place?"

It's in Bel Air, at a friend's house." Now this man had my attention, talking about a Bible study in a home in Bel Air. This I had to see, because I thought most rich people in that city were Jewish and never talk about religion.

Thursday night arrived, and I decided to take my daughter, Shawna, with me to the Bible study. When I arrived at the house in Bel Air, we were greeted with a smile and a big hug. I saw the gentleman who invited me. He was so surprised I actually came. I still did not know why I wanted to go to this Bible study. The spirit of God was drawing me there. A deep sense of peace enveloped me. Then the music began, with a young man singing and playing a guitar. I just listened and watched. I needed to know why these people were so kind and loving, and had glows on their faces. This was the same glow I saw in the faces of Nancy's daughters when they worked in the spa.

After the music was over, Al Kasha, the owner of the home, began to share the Bible with us. He was a born-again Jew, who was big in the entertainment industry. He was a composer who won a few Oscars and other awards. He loved God with all his heart! I was dumbfounded by what I heard and saw. Most of the people there, including myself, were in the entertainment field. Was this for real?

Another person took the time to explain the beauty of why everyone came to these studies and invited me to church. I jumped at the chance to go. The church was called The Hiding Place and was only three blocks from my apartment in Westwood. As I approached the doors of a high school auditorium, music was blasting. *Do I have the right place?* I wondered. *Is that why it's called The Hiding Place, because it's at a high school?* The man who invited me greeted me at the door. The place was filled with young people, and everyone seemed so happy. It was nothing like the Catholic churches I had attended. It was more like a holy nightclub.

I must confess I was very involved in private nightclubs in Beverly Hills, choreographing fashion shows. And that is where all the good-looking people went to meet and have fun. The nightlife was my outlet to feel free, covering up my insecurities and looking for attention in a positive way. I loved dancing!

The young, charismatic pastor at The Hiding Place was also the worship leader, and the sound of his voice opened my heart to Jesus. This Jesus seemed alive and well. I needed to know more about Him, not Mary or the saints, but Jesus! My hearing loss made it difficult to hear what the pastor was preaching. I started putting bits and pieces together, but I was still not able to understand everything. It was frustrating because it was difficult to read the pastor's lips while he was preaching his message. I could feel the Spirit of God in the church. I cried for weeks every time I visited there. I just had to do the best I could by reading the Bible. God was real!

Another Playboy?

Four months later, I was at one of the nightclubs with my girlfriend. I felt someone staring at me, and when I turned in his direction, our eyes caught each other's. I became shy. I thought, *He's cute, young, but looks like a playboy. No, this is the wrong kind of man for me. I am just asking for more heartache.* But he kept staring. I left my seat to go to the ladies room, and when leaving, I looked over and saw him point his finger at me. He motioned for me to come to him. Liking the attention he was giving me, I went over. We exchanged phone numbers that evening. Two days later, I called him. "I knew you would call," he said as he answered the phone. I laughed and realized he was arrogant. What did I want with someone like him? But it didn't take long before I found myself crazy about him. With his heavy Jordanian accent and his tendency to talk very fast, I found it difficult to read his lips. His words seemed to run together. Now what do I do to make this relationship compatible? Communication was a bit difficult with him.

A New Man

We had similar career goals and could complement each other. Jim was a photographer, and I was a model and makeup artist. I saw a future with this man. Besides, I had prayed in church, asking God to bring me a man I could grow with in the things of the Lord. I had made a mess out of choosing the wrong men in the past. It was time to let God be a factor in my future choices regarding the men in my life. At this time, though, I was not thinking he was from God. God allowed me to go through the hard times in order to show me that I was going about this relationship the wrong way.

After dating for six months, Jim tried to find a way to break up with me. He never wanted to be in a relationship longer than three months. He had his own single-minded goals in life, and marriage was not one of them. He had a list of nevers, like never get married, never have children, never have pets, never, never, never. Jim was difficult to deal with, and I went through much heartache because I was going ahead of God. I was not walking in obedience to the Lord. Later in the relationship, God used me to bring Jim to Jesus. That was a miracle!

Jim decided to stay in the relationship, and we formed a new business, Steele Productions. He was good at photography, and I was a good makeup artist and stylist. This gave us a chance to get to know each other better and to build a business together. I had to work harder to communicate with him because of his foreign accent.

I knew deep inside this relationship would not last unless I took him to church to be saved. I was living with him in sin and going to church on Sundays. What kind of Christian was I? I was a carnal, selfish, lustful Christian, trying to do it my way. And Jim was doing it his way, while also confessing he knew God. Our relationship got worse and worse because I wasn't able to say no to Jim about sex and living together. God withdrew His peace from me because I was not putting Him first in my life. Breaking away from a sexual relationship with someone you love may be one of the hardest things for a teenager or any woman to do.

I hope as you read my confession you will learn something and save yourself the trials and hardships that lead to despair. Obeying the Word is so much more gratifying than pleasing your flesh. I learned the hard way, and hope you will seek God's will for your life. Romans 6:12 (NKJV) says, **"Therefore, do not let sin reign in your mortal body, that you should obey it in its lusts."**

One day Jim and I got in a terrible argument. He was angry to the point of walking out on me. I was finished with trying to make the relationship work, and it did not matter to me that he was leaving. But something very interesting happened. As I sat on the couch, something prompted me to go after him and say, "Wait, God sent you to me." We both looked at each other, dumbfounded and shocked at the words that tumbled from my mouth. We both felt the Spirit of God when I said that. Jim had not experienced the Holy Spirit, because he had not received the Lord into his heart. God was about to do something far more than what I prayed for.

A few months passed, and I was still miserable in this relationship. I ran to God in tears, and He spoke to me, saying, "You must change first. Your sin is a stumbling block to the salvation of Jim. Obey my Word." I had to change first in order to have a happy and peaceful life. God had to change me before I could bring people to Christ. I was a bad example as a Christian, and no one would come to know Him with this sin in my life. Because of my hearing loss and not able to hear all the preacher taught us, I was perishing for lack of knowledge. I was also not reading the Bible. The Word of God—the Bible—is alive and will transform your way of thinking, and I had to discipline myself if I wanted to be a disciple of Christ. I needed to deny myself and follow Christ. It was time for me to lay down all my plans, relationships, and needs in order to receive God's best for me.

My Transformation

It was time for me to get away from Jim for a while and make some serious decisions. The church I had attended for three years had arranged for a three-day camping trip to Mt. Baldy. I had never gone camping before. Somehow I knew this was going to be a turning point in my life, and I was so desperate to find a new way. I invited Jim, hoping he would go so he could get saved, but he refused to go. God planned this trip for me and my eleven-year-old daughter, Shawna.

I had never seen such a beautiful site. There were unforgettable camp fires every night and wonderful anointed worship. Who would ever believe there was a heaven on earth? It was, and I was amazed. The Spirit of God began to move in a mighty way. The group leader surrounded me with a few others to pray for me. For the first time, I felt my heart being healed of the hurts of my past and from the disappointments I had with Jim. My daughter and I cried all night with joy, knowing God was healing us. The Holy Spirit was cleansing our souls from all the emotional abuse we had been through. God brought my daughter and I closer together, so we could start a new life in Him. My life was being transformed! I was filled with the Spirit and His power. Darkness could no longer hold me down. I was set free to move on with the calling on my life to share the love of Jesus with others. I was so excited about life.

Now it was time to head back down to the big city, where life can be so disappointing. Being on the mountaintop, where the stars are shining, the air is refreshing, and the silence is so peaceful. My life would never be the same.

Facing Reality

As I drove home, all I could think about was my love for Jesus. He set me free and gave me real love. When I arrived at my apartment,

Jim was sitting on the couch. The first words I said to him were, "Jim, we can't have sex anymore. I am serving the Lord 100 percent!" Jim did not say one word to me, because he could see something had changed in me. "You're moving all your belongings to the other bedroom. And start thinking about moving out," I told him. He did what I asked but wondered what had happened to me.

Taking this first step was the best thing I have ever done in my life. I was obeying God and trusting Him to lead me on the right path. He created us to be in His image and likeness. We just do not know it, because we are blinded by the cares of this world and the distraction of the Devil. I have also found my true father. God revealed to me during this time that He is my Father. I am no longer a fatherless child but a daughter of God. I became a daddy's girl again, crying out, "Abba. Father!" **"And because you are sons [and daughters], God has sent forth the Spirit of His Son into your hearts, crying out, 'Abba Father!'"** (Galatians 4:6-7 NKJV)

Time was moving fast, and every night I was in fellowship with strong Christians disciplined in the Word of God. Jim could see I was very happy and thought I had met a new man. He did not know what happen at the camping trip. I did meet a new man, and His name is Jesus Christ. All he knew was I came home changed! I was free from all the cares of this world. God had a plan for me—and for Jim.

Dreams and Visions

One month after my camping trip experience, while Jim was sleeping, he had a visitation from God. He was taken back in time to where Christ was crucified. He saw this man nailed to the cross, and their eyes met for the first time. Jim felt naked before him and realized the man on the cross knew everything about him. Jim woke from his sleep troubled by what he saw.

Jim went to his father's house that afternoon, and his father had had a dream also. He saw Jesus in a bright white robe. His father said to Jesus, "How can I tell people that I have seen You?" Jesus gave him a ring in the dream, like no other. When Jim's father tried to put it on, it did not fit. Suddenly, he woke from the dream, with his finger on one hand trying to put on a ring. He wondered why Jesus would give him a ring that did not fit. After he thought about it, he came to the conclusion the ring represented a son, and one of his sons was not fitted to do what He wanted. Jim was in awe of his father's dream and needed to know the meaning of it all.

Jim felt led to visit his faithful, praying aunt. "You are persecuting Jesus by living in sin with Trish. You should marry her, for she is a good woman." Jim got upset, told her off, and left.

The next morning, Jim asked to go to church with me. I told him, "Do it for God, not for me." In the past, he would only go to church to satisfy me and make me think he was somewhat godly.

Jim got mad and said, "I'm not doing this for you!" He left to drive himself to church. I arrived at the church before he did. I guess he had a hard time finding The Hiding Place. Music was playing when Jim came in. He stood beside me and humbled himself. He raised his hands up. God had captured Jim's heart, and he was never the same.

The Marriage Setup

A few weeks later, Jim and I were in church together, and the pastor began to talk about premarital classes for those who thinking about getting married. **"Being confident of this very thing, that He who began a good work in you will complete it until the day of Jesus Christ"** (Philippians 1:6 NKJV). Jim and I took the classes together.

Three months later, just after we finished the classes, our wedding was planned in one week. Off to Vegas we went with a few friends; our immediate family met us there. It was a quick wedding that left me wondering if I did the right thing. We all dream to meet our perfect mate and have a beautiful wedding, but that was not the case for us. I now had a marriage and mate picked by God. We had no idea how much work was needed to put our past behind us and make our marriage work.

Marriage: The Two Shall become One Flesh

[6]"But from the beginning of the creation, God made them male and female, [7]For this reason a man shall leave his father and mother and be joined to his wife, [8]and the two shall become one flesh; so then they are no longer two, but one flesh." (Mark 10:6-8 NKJV)

The first three years of our marriage were very hard for us both. We wanted to abandon the marriage many times, but God convicted us of our wrong. We did not have the normal marriage most Christian people do. We had to fight our flesh every day, making it our slave, so Christ may be formed in us. Some people do not understand the mysteries of a successful marriage. It takes work and obedience to God's purpose and plan for your life. We needed to be one in our thinking, goals, and purposes. Two broken and dysfunctional people do not make a whole. They make a mess.

God was faithful in beginning a good work in my husband and me. He began doing a series of miracles in both of our lives. Part of our biggest problem was the language barrier between us. Jim was willing to go to school and take English classes to get rid of his accent and to learn how to read English. But the Holy Spirit taught Jim how to read English through reading the Bible every day for months. This Bible transformed his life and delivered him from all bad habits. If we were going to become one flesh in this marriage, we had to surrender all our faults and sin to the Lord. The Word of God and obedience to it did allow the miracles to manifest in our life.

God performed miracles in my life as well, especially restoring 70 percent of my hearing loss. My speech impediment began to clear up, and now when I preach, my speech becomes close to prefect. Jesus also had to heal all my emotional scars caused by past abuse and disappointing relationships.

Married Life

After six months of marriage and having Bible studies in our home, we decided to host Christian music concerts called 'Concerts with a Vision.' I was deeply involved in the entertainment industry and sought Christian artists to sing at our events. Darrell Mansfield, who played the part of Jesus in the video for which I worked as the makeup artist, had an incredible voice and anointing on his life. It impacted me so much that I knew one day I would see him again. When I called on him to sing at an event, his wife answered. She asked, "Who is this?" I told her my name. She paused and then asked, "Is this the Trish who worked with my mother at Jack LaLanne Health Spa?"

Then it dawned on me she must be one of Nancy's daughters, and immediately I said, "Yes. And where is your mother?" We were reunited, and God answered Nancy's prayers. God used people Nancy had known for years to minister to me and preserve me. God used her prayer to do a full circle of restoration.

Called to Ministry

Just after we married, Jim and I were invited to a Bible study/fellowship with twelve people in the room. We met a man named Scott who spoke about the cross of Jesus Christ. He shared on the subject of the gifts of the Holy Spirit. Then my husband noticed one of our friends was filled with the Holy Spirit and received her spiritual language. My husband said, "I want that!"

Jim was asked, "Have you been baptized in the Holy Spirit?" Some had not heard of such a thing. My husband said he thought he had. "No, you would know you have by receiving your spiritual language in other tongues," Scott explained. "Jim, humble yourself, and I'll pray for you to receive."

Immediately, a rushing of mighty tongues in a language only God could understand flowed from my husband's lips. Jim's spiritual language gushed forth all night, and his countenance changed. It was a night of miracles for everyone present as God blessed us with the manifestation of all the gifts of the Holy Spirit. I suggest you read 1 Corinthians chapter 12 to understand the manifestations of the Holy Spirit gifts.

The evening's excitement left us wanting more! My husband and I wanted to grow in the things of the Lord. We were growing together in God's Word and in His ministry. Our mutual growth in Christ was so rapid that our life took a 180-degree turn quite quickly. I thank God for a husband teaching me the Word as we learned to follow God's plan. God began to turn Jim's weakness into strengths and he was growing into a powerful preacher so many lives could be touched, saved and healed. We were once foolish and now wise in God. "But God hath chosen the foolish things of the world to confound the wise; and God hath chosen the weak things of the world to confound the things which are mighty" (1 Corinthians 1:27).

A New Chapter in Our Lives

Three years quickly passed leading Bible studies, where the power of God transformed lives, including ours. God wanted to do more with us, but we were not sure if we would be ready for it. Jim had said in the past that he never wanted to marry, never wanted children, never, never, never. But with God, all things are possible. God spoke, "I want to bless you with a child. Now is the time." Jim really had to pray about this. It was another part of his flesh he had to give up.

A new chapter in our life was about to begin, and we started planning. My daughter, Shawna, was finally going to have a sister or brother after seventeen years of hoping. I was forty years old at the time, and most people felt I was too old to have a child. No, my age was symbolic of leaving the wilderness and entering into the Promised land. This Promise Land was the new chapter forever. Before our child was born, God gave us dreams and many words about our new baby. In the most profound dream, I saw myself in the hospital bed, holding a baby. My husband was standing next to me and holding another baby. So we thought we were going to have twins. Everywhere I went I saw twins. My husband and I thought that would be wonderful, a double blessing. But when we found out I was pregnant with only one child, I asked God, "Did I miss something in the dream?" God said to me, "Here are your twins."

During the beginning of my pregnancy, Jim and I were asked to meet with the district supervisor of the Foursquare International Church. We had been recommended to be assistant ministers at a small church we attended. As we spoke with the supervisor, the Holy Spirit directed him to a new plan. We were not to be assistants to the pastors, which had brought us there, but to be head pastors of our own church. We were not sure, because we were not looking to be in full-time ministry. This was a setup from God, and only He could make this happen. It was time to take our Bible studies into a church building and pastor people.

At the same time we needed to choose a hospital to have our child and a location for the church, and it happened to be in the same city. So, two births were about to take place—our baby and our church. Both of them were being birthed in Woodland Hills in the same year. The dream became very clear to me. I was holding one baby (Michelle), and Jim held the other baby (True Life Ministries).

Raising a Family

I have so many good memories of my pregnancy and the birthing of our new church. I never thought the day would come for me to be a mother again and start a new family. As I looked back at my life and saw how messed up it was, who would think it could be restored to such a good future? God is truly in the restoration business (Isaiah 54:1–2 NKJV).

At the grand opening of our church, the love of God touched many hearts. We were happy to see everyone experience the power of the Holy Spirit. We had new visitors every week. Many of them came from the Bible study we had for three years. Most of them became like children to us. We wanted to be like responsible parents and raise them up in the Word, teaching them what the Holy Spirit had taught us.

My Calling to Preach

My husband's zeal and love for God inspired so many people, including me. I could see he had a deep love for the Lord and wanted to please Him in every way.

Jim kept asking me to start a women's Bible study at home. But I was uncomfortable with that because I still had a mild speech impairment, hearing loss, and lack of biblical knowledge. The Word of God needs to be understood very carefully and not taken lightly. As pastors in the Foursquare denomination, we were required to attend conferences and meetings every year. We attended a conference at Jack Hayford's church, where there were hundreds of pastors from all over the world. My husband and I were praising God through the worship music when suddenly, the Lord said to me, "I have called you to teach women and help them."

I responded, "But I do not speak well enough and have no teaching skills."

The Lord said, "I will speak through you, and the Holy Spirit will teach." I began to cry like a baby. His words and presence humbled me as I agreed to do it.

Women Crowned in Glory was the name God gave me for our women's ministry. **"You shall be a crown of glory in the hand of the Lord, and a royal diadem in the hand of your God"** (Isaiah 62:3 NKJV). I was so surprised to find that Scripture and use it as the model verse for our ministry.

The Lord reminded me of the beauty pageant I had won five years ago as Mrs. California, and spoke to my heart: "The discipline that it took for you to win the California state pageant is the same discipline I want you to teach the women. Make disciples and crown them with My love."

Trish Steele as Mrs. California

Life was getting better and better as I stepped out to minister, teaching women how to feel beautiful from the inside out. I was able to use all my talents as a makeup artist, wardrobe stylist, hairstylist, fashion show choreographer, craft designer, fashion show choreographer, and now with 'Women Crowned In Glory, Inc.'

Healing the Brokenhearted

How do women heal from years of abuse and disappointments? Many women have asked this question; many others have buried this question. Some have a miraculous healing, while some take years of counseling.

Being a minister taught me so much about the healing power of God. After my own experience of abuse, rejection, and ridicule, I had a heart that needed healing from anger, denial, and more. But God delivered me from them all and healed my heart. Some healings happened instantly, others healed overnight, still other healings needed much more time.

God promised us the Lord Jesus came to heal all the brokenness in our life. In order to receive the Lord's healing we must first receive Him who paid the price for our healing and our salvation. That is Jesus Christ.

This is the time for confessions! We must confess our sins to each other in order to be healed. I speak of the deep wounds people have carried in their hearts for years. The Spirit of the Lord is here now and forever to heal the brokenhearted and set the captives free from depression, suicide and addiction and every form of emotional wound and issue. My husband and I have spent many nights praying and casting out unclean spirits keeping people in bondage.

The Need for Forgiveness

In the process of getting healed we must forgive those who hurt us. Forgiveness can be the hardest thing for most people because they find unforgiveness gives them power to protect their emotions. It is like putting a wall up to protect you from ever getting hurt again. But this wall hinders you from moving forward to a new life.

Jesus gave His love and died for us that we may pick up our cross and follow Him. His is the greatest love, and His love will never fail. My husband and I learned more about His love through our sufferings in our relationship over the years. Love grows deeper every year as we go through new trials. Those trials deepen our roots in the heart of God. **"By this all will know that you are My disciples, if you have love for one another"** (John 13:35 NKJV).

Walking by Faith

In the first two years of my husband's walk with the Lord, he was able to be sustained through disability benefits. They allowed him hours and hours for reading and learning the Word of God. I had a hard time understanding this because he was a hard worker and staying home all day seemed like wasted time. I had no idea what God was doing with Jim. But the Lord was teaching me to rely on Him for everything. During that time, we had to believe God would supply our needs. One income and his disability were not enough to pay the rent and bills we had. But God opened the door for my husband to teach Bible studies in our home, so extra income came in to cover our bills. Now that is faith with works.

As mentioned previously, We held Bible studies in our home for three years. After the first year, Jim went back to work. Again God open that door and had him do unfinished business there. Jim had to go back to pray and share the love of Jesus to these hard-core men who mocked him for this faith. He experienced the same rejection Jesus faced. This was a short season of employment for Jim, for God was pleased with him for not being ashamed of the gospel he shared at work.

God began to talk to my husband about living by faith again. Jim was sitting in his car, spending time with God alone, while I worked in the house. After a few hours, I walked out to the car and saw my husband still praying. Jim took a moment and said to me, "God wants me to quit my job."

I asked, "Right before the holidays He wants you to quit?" My husband said yes. I told him I wasn't comfortable with that. Besides, he just got his job back six months before. Christmas was just two months away. I was not happy about this decision. Just as I was walking away, Mr. and Mrs. Bentley, who were part of our Bible studies, came outside to tell Jim God told them to give us money to start our nonprofit corporation, The Kingdom of God on Earth Ministry. My husband was awestruck because that was the confirmation we needed to hear at that moment! God enabled Jim to quit his job with comfort. This couple was in our life to support the ministry at a crucial moment of our ministry.

Every year we loved to go shopping for the holidays and give family gifts to express the blessing of Jesus' birth. Jim came from a family of nine brothers and sisters. I came from a family of five brothers and sisters. Neither of our parents had received the Lord, and they felt we had become too religious for them.

This Christmas we had no money to shop for gifts for our family members. Two days before Christmas, I was ready to call my mother to tell her we would not be attending the family Christmas gathering, because we had no gifts to bring. I was not self-pitying. I just did not want to give my family the opportunity to mock Jesus, because He had not provided for us to come with gifts.

"Wait, put the phone down," said Jim when I was about to cancel my attendance. "Let's pray about this." So I put down the phone down, and we prayed God would provide what He wanted us to have. My husband's obedience and our agreeing in prayer allowed God an opportunity to do a miracle.

There was a knock at the door just one hour after we prayed. I was at the grocery store. My husband answered the door and there was a friend of ours. He said, "I was praying this morning to God. I told God I want to give out of my treasures to bless someone for Christmas. God said go to Jim and Trish's home and give them whatever they need." I came home shortly after our friend arrived and he shared with me what the Lord told him to do. This friend opens a big suitcase full of silver jewelry and said, "Take as much as you want for all your family members and close friends. The more you take, the more I will be blessed."

On Christmas Day, Jim and I went to my family's home and shared the story. "I was going to call and cancel because we had no money to buy gifts. But God sent a special person to bless you! This person told me to select any piece of jewelry for each of you, because God told him to do it because He loves you. God cares more about you and your Christmas than I do." My family was in awe, and some of them got tears in their eyes because the love of God was there to confirm His Word.

My Daughters

It is very rewarding to have children, especially when they are doing well for themselves. We all want the best for our children. We give them good advice and hope they will use it. But for some reason, they think we are just a little too old fashioned. So they start making their own decisions and often going in the wrong direction.

My first daughter, Shawna, had been raised half her life with her grandparents and half the time with me. After the separation, Shawna got the best care at her grandparents' home. They provided for her in abundance—the best private schools, best vacations, and the best home. She was very athletic and did sports well. She also got honors in her sports and was able to travel to Europe for baseball competitions. I was so proud of her and her achievements. She was a wonderful child and never had any problems growing up, even when she lived with me off and on over the years.

By the time Shawna went to college, her Christian walk did not have enough roots to keep her grounded. The parties and lust that occurred on campus turned her life upside down. Her life has not been the same since. She did graduate with her bachelor's degree in business and became successful in her field of work. But her relationship with Jesus was gone.

Now we have my second daughter, Michelle, who is another story and lesson to be learned. Michelle was our promised baby, and she was raised in a Christian home and in church every week. At home, we always had people over for prayer and Bible studies. Her life was filled with love, excitement, traveling, fun, and laughter. She was a happy girl, full of energy. Michelle also had a deep voice and a great laugh. Many people got so much joy out of hearing her laugh.

School was not easy for Michelle, and she had to try extra hard to pass her classes with Cs or better. I spent a lot of time teaching her and making sure she got the best of care at her public school. I established good relationships with the teachers, and they shared wonderful reports about Michelle.

Michelle was about to enter middle school, and one of the teachers was concerned about her making this transition from grammar school. She said, "I am concerned about Michelle going to this school and not being able to get along with the other students." When I asked why she said, "She seems so naïve and innocent, that she may not adapt well with her classmates and the way they act may hinder her." They thought she was very sheltered from the world. Yes, she was sheltered from many things of this world, and I was not going to expose her to all that junk on TV as well as many of the kids who behaved so rudely.

Michelle's Mountain

Michelle was about to face a big mountain ahead of her. I had no idea children today could be so cruel and mean to one another. She wanted out of that school, and there was nothing I could do. It was the best public school with the best teachers, classes, and opportunities to excel in learning. As ministers of a small church, we did not have funds to hire a tutor for her. Nor did I feel led to homeschool her.

It came down to why my daughter was being picked on. I am sure many parents have to deal with this, and my heart goes out to them all. They ridicule and bully the innocent students when they first arrive. Today, the PTA addresses these subjects in the schools. That was not the case when Michelle needed it, though.

After the first four months of attending a new school, I noticed her personality was changing. Her attitude toward me became harsh. She thought I did not care about her opinions. My heart and faith were being tested. "God, where are you in this?" I asked. "How can you let this happen to Michelle?" I only got one answer for my Michelle, and it was growing pains. She was making the big transition from a child to teenager along, which included all the hormonal changes bodies have to go through. My baby was no longer a baby but turning into a teen. She was growing up.

As the years went by, Michelle became an excellent student and discovered the gifts that best expressed her personality. She took drawing and art classes. At home, we did a lot of crafts and sewed by hand special items to raise funds for the church. I noticed she had a gift and desire to become a fashion designer, so we bought her a sewing machine at the age of thirteen. Now she had the tools to become more creative.

Michelle and I started a new fashion line called 'Cover Me Wear' by Michelle Steele. Some of the garments were made of furry, warm, thick fabrics to cover the shoulders or chest to keep warm. The fashions were shaped like ponchos and could be worn over any garment or swimsuit. They were fashionable for people of all ages, shapes, and sizes. I was able to get my daughter a write up in a magazine called *Celebrity Society*. I was so proud of her, and we were working well together as a team.

Middle school was over, and Michelle was about to go to High School. What would the world hold for her now? It was a totally opposite environment for her. She was respected and liked by her peers who saw her designs in the fashion show on campus. This fashion show happens every year, and many students have talents and opportunities to make it in the fashion industry. Michelle was the only ninth-grader able to participate because she had established herself the year before with the Cover Me wear designs.

When I was a teenager, I designed and sewed clothing. I loved designing and sewing new looks for myself. I wanted to become a fashion designer, but no one mentored me or encouraged me to do so. I was able to lead and guide her and give her the support she needed as a fashion designer. Her dream was and is being fulfilled.

When Michelle entered her junior year of high school, new changes were being made in her classes. They required her to study very hard in order to pass the requirements for her to graduate. She would get up every morning at 6:00 a.m. to be at school by 7:00 a.m. to meet with one of the teachers, who privately tutored her. The classes she was taking were hard for her. But she wanted to stay in them and was determined to pass.

Michelle met a new group of friends by attending these classes. And this was where many problems began. Many of these teens had a different lifestyle than our family. My daughter wanted to be like them, thinking she would gain popularity. She was already popular with her group of friends, so I didn't know why she wanted to change her lifestyle to something that did not edify God. It is a shame teenagers take on many ungodly forms, and we cannot control their decision and choices.

The Wrong Friends

Michelle began to associate with the wrong group of teens. I noticed she was losing a lot of weight. She also was not sleeping much, and she had mood swings. She seemed hardened and distant from me. She sometimes became very sick, and the school would call me to come and pick her up. I knew her life was falling apart, and I took her to the hospital to be checked out. The doctors said she was dehydrated and needed to eat. Then the nurse recommended I take her to a psychologist for therapy. I was devastated with the doctor's report. My little girl was entangled with ungodly teens.

Just a few days after her last visit to the hospital, Michelle started imagining things and seeing spiritual beings that were evil. She had a breakdown, and we had to call for help. I had never experienced such a problem, and my faith was shattered. *How can God allow this to happen?* I wondered. Michelle's life was taken captive by an evil force, and we had to fight to get her back. She ended up in the hospital.

Her father and I went daily to the hospital to pray for her and spent hours giving her love and the Word of God. There were other teens at this hospital as well. We were shocked to discover so many were there for attempting suicide. This was not my daughter's case, but she was being tormented by evil spirits.

The hospital was a big opportunity to minister to the teens and parents. For five months Michelle lived in a special dorm at the hospital. We were allowed to talk to the other teens and minister to them about the love of Jesus. No one could stop what God was doing in this place. We met numerous other Christian teens and prayed for them. Many were touched and healed.

As Michelle was coming out of the darkness, all she could say was, "Daddy, keep on praying for me. I am a new baby, and you need to teach me how to be a minister." This was so profound, and only the Holy Spirit could say this through her. While Michelle was in the hospital, she started praying for the teens to be delivered from demons, because she could see them. God was using her in a big way to show us that He had His hands on her, and she would be healed according to His timing.

As parents, we frequently ask, "Where did we go wrong," in raising our children. Often it is not the parents who do wrong, but the children who act out foolishly. Thank God He works all things together for good for those who love Him. Now Michelle has a testimony to share, which many teens and young adults will hear and hopefully be saved. God transforms those who trust and believe in Him from darkness to His glorious Light!

Shawna Sherburne, Trish Steele, and Michelle Steele, all work as a team to help Safe Passage and host fundraising events.

Women's Ministry

I mentioned in a previous chapter that God wanted me to start a women's ministry. When the time comes for God to use us, He will give us much grace! We must follow God's leading and that is usually in a territory that is unfamiliar to you. We must be strong in faith and know that whatever good work He begins in us He will be faithful to complete.

I had to see myself as a queen who had the mantle of the royal kingdom. My years of beauty pageant experience taught me to understand the order and discipline it takes to win the crown. Pageants have certain guidelines, and you must abide by them to qualify as a contestant. Jesus has guidelines in His Word that one must follow to qualify as a disciple. I heard the Lord say, "The discipline that it took for you to win the California state pageant is the same discipline I want you to teach the women, making them glorious with My crown of glory." He wanted me to use every gift and talent for His glory!

It came time to prepare workshops, women's retreats, and speaking engagements for Women Crowned in Glory. We had women of all ages, from all walks of life, and from different countries. I was very grateful for the talented and wonderful team of women God sent to my ministry to help me prepare for the new 'queens' that are to be crowned in His glory. It was a team of experts in their fields that had the anointing of God flowing out of them and transforming the women. Just as in the book of Esther, where there was a team of people who worked with the women to prepare them for the role of queen. But in this case, many women were being crowned as queen.

Women Crowned in Glory

The Women Crowned in Glory ministry was filled with God's love and signs and wonders for over eight years. Then it was time for me to conquer another kingdom, a kingdom of those who were under the sway of the Devil. Women and children suffering from domestic violence and escaping to shelters are under this dark kingdom. There are two kingdoms; the kingdom of God and the kingdom of darkness (the Devil's territory). God wanted me to go out and minister at women's shelters.

Before I headed out to the shelters, I made sure I had a partner God ordained for me to work with. He sends His ministers out in twos because together they are much more powerful. I had established a life-changing program for abused women called Stepping Stones to a New Life. I was excited about this new thing God was doing in my life. Going to shelters and ministering in Jesus name to the hearts of women, abused and crying for help, was and is very rewarding. I know the principle of establishing

God's kingdom, and I was on a mission. I knew the authority I have in Christ and that authority would break down the gates of the Devil's kingdom.

In the spring of 1995, a very talented artist named Lidia Penczar, who painted beautifully, saw a vision of Women Crowned in Glory in which there were twelve women on their knees before Jesus. They were wearing unusually draped gowns over their bodies, that looked angelic. On their heads were crowns, and each woman's crown were different in size, shape, and in color, which represented their rewards. Jesus was in His glorified body and there to crown each woman accordingly. This vision was given to her to paint for my ministry.

Lidia went to her little studio and found a white board and color pencils. "Now take what you have, and use it to draw the vision. Do not stop until it is done," Jesus said. As the Holy Spirit led her, the vision became clearer, and the drawing became more glorious. The scene resembles the *Last Supper*, but it's called the *Marriage Supper of the Lamb*. God enabled Lidia to draw something she'd never done before. I still have the drawing in a gold frame, hanging in my office. Every time I look it, I think of all the rewards Jesus has for those who do the will of the Father. I cannot do it justice with words, such is its incredible beautiful.

Three years later, Women Crowned in Glory published its own book, *The Compelling Life Changing Stories of 12 Women*. Lidia's painting was printed in this book. I am a blessed woman to have taken part in this book. It helps women learn how to come to God with their problems, tragedies, sorrows, and victories. The women in this book share how they allowed our heavenly Father to put their lives back together and make them a whole person with a new life.

By God's divine providence, I believe I met each and every woman for the purpose of the book. All twelve of us writing our stories were doing our best to live in His righteousness, knowledge, and love. We were once dull stones, but the master, Jesus Christ, chose us to be refined through fire that we may be radiant and valuable for His kingdom.

Safe Passage

In the year 2000, our dear friends from Greece, helped me to establish my ministry. I took Women Crowned in Glory (WCIG) and incorporated it as a nonprofit. Everything I learned in ministry with True Life Church (my husband's church) was a stepping-stone to a new mission to evangelize in the marketplace. WCIG was doing great and transforming lives, bringing women to be healed and live a new life in Christ. I was ready to step out of the boat and into the water by faith.

I renamed WCIG to Safe Passage. It transforms the lives of abused women and their children to a new and better life by providing hope, opportunity, and empowerment.

Many in the world do not comprehend the spiritual things of God and His work. Not many want to hear about God or Jesus Christ. In fact, it is often against the rules of a business or shelter. Some people are so hardened that they get turned off by hearing the name of Jesus. Again, preparation is so important when going out to ask for funds from corporations, foundations, and individuals. God has been faithful to give me favor and open many doors with people, in high positions.

Once I get into the door of women's shelters, the opportunity and His favor come to share the vision of Safe Passage through my testimony. I come as one like them, who understands domestic violence. I share with them how God blessed me to start this mission, because He loves them so much and wants to make them whole.

Our new program, Stepping-Stone to a New Life, started in June 2001. This program is a "life makeover" from the inside out, offering restorative health service, counseling, corrective dental and plastic surgery to remove the scars and damage due to the abuse, job resources, help finding a new residence with donated furnishings, and follow-up sources. Over fifteen hundred women and their children in the past thirteen years have come to Safe Passage for help, and God has proved His great love for them through this.

I often wonder why haven't more churches opened their doors to organizations such as Safe Passage? Why do people turn their heads the other way, as if domestic violence doesn't exist? I have approached many churches with this question.

Cycles of Abuse

Let me share with you the cycle of abuse that leads to domestic violence. It is called power to control. *Intimidation:* putting someone in fear through looks, actions, gestures, speaking loudly, smashing things, or destroying property. *Threats:* making and carrying out threats to do something to hurt another emotionally or physically. For example, threatening to take the children, commit suicide, or report another to welfare services. *Emotional Abuse*: putting another down or making someone feel bad about himself or herself; calling another person names. Making another think he or she is crazy; playing mind games. *Physical Abuse:* punching, kicking, grabbing, using a weapon, beating, throwing him or her down, twisting arms, tripping, biting, pushing, shoving, hitting, slapping, choking, pulling hair. *Sexual Abuse:* Sexual action against another person's will. Physically attacking the sexual parts of another's body or treating someone like a sex object. *Isolation:* controlling what another person does, who he or she sees and talks to, and where someone goes. *Economic Abuse:* trying to keep another person from getting or keeping a job, making him or her ask for money, or taking his or her money.

Safe Passage's mission is to transform the lives of many. We pray we will have the opportunity to meet and serve individuals in need with our anointed program, Stepping Stones to a New Life.

In the past thirteen years, Safe Passage has had a 95 percent success rate with the women and children who go through our program. I have seen wonderful miracles and salvation for every woman who has gone through the program, enabling them to forgive those who abused them and be set free and move on to a new life. All these women have accepted Jesus as their Savior. They truly know God has kept them from being destroyed. "Love covers a multitude of sins."

The Good News, There's Help!

"And we know that all things work together for good to those who love God, to those who are called according to His purpose" (Romans 8:28 NKJV). Everything in our past, present, and future will be used for God's plans.Jim and I have seen God come through for us in our trials, and He has given us grace, love and forgiveness to help others. We look forward to the future and all that God has in store for us and how He will use us in the lives of others. As Kings and Queens, we will rule and reign with Him on earth and in Heaven. Hallelujah!

Trish Steele
Women Crowned in Glory Inc./Safe Passage
P. O. Box 40034,
Studio City, CA 91604
www.safepassagelives.org
818-232-7476

Jim and Trish Steele have been married for twenty-five years and minister wherever they are called.

True Life Kingdom Ministry www.truelifekingdom.org

Jim Steele

Deborah Parker

"The Lord is there to rescue all who are discouraged and have given up hope." Psalm 34:18 (Contemporary English Version)

I'm sharing my story with you in the hope it will help you. We all have skeletons in our closets, and hope no one will discover them. In writing this, I would never want to hurt anyone or uncover family secrets. Nor will I claim I am the only victim. Every perpetrator was once a victim.

Early Years

My life of fear and abandonment began when I was a baby. My parents divorced, and I never knew my father. I was told he was a very handsome man in the entertainment industry and unhappy at home. He found another woman and left my mom heartbroken, with two daughters to raise alone.

When I was about four years old, she met and married another man. Within a very short time, she became pregnant again. They decided to leave California and move to New York to start a new life. We moved in with my aunt and uncle and their family until my stepfather found work. But before she delivered my brother, this man also left. One day he went looking for a job and never returned home. With this second failed attempt to find love, my mother fell into utter despair. She now had three children and no husband.

No matter what age we are, I think we all have the ability to block out our emotions and memories like they've never happened. Whatever sadness and feelings of abandonment I may have felt, I don't remember them. I found out in my adult years from my aunt that I was very sad when my stepfather left us.

California, Here We Come!

From left to right: my Grandmother, mother, sister, cousin Carol, Deborah and my brother

Several months after my brother was born, my mother, sister, and I returned to California. Once we were settled, my grandmother joined us, bringing my baby brother with her. She lived with us to help care for us kids while mom worked. My grandmother was such a tremendous strength to our family. While Mom worked, she ran the house like a well-oiled machine. She never missed a beat and always seemed to know what was going on in our lives. I felt secure in her arms, and she brought a lot of comfort to me. She had a way of making me feel everything would be okay. She was devoted to God and her family. She loved Jesus with her whole heart. She was one of the most talented women I've ever known. She crocheted with thread beautifully, creating the most exquisite designs. Her attention to detail was astonishing. She also knitted, embroidered, and was passionate about cooking. If a guest dropped by, my grandmother would go into that kitchen and prepare a wonderful meal from scratch. That is one gift the entire family inherited from her. She had a genuine love for people and was always ready to serve and help. My grandmother was a jewel in my life that birthed a treasure in my heart for the meaning of family.

During those early years, I barely saw my mom, because she worked two jobs to support us. But she sometimes came home between breaks to take me to see the horses that lived nearby, and we'd eat lunch together. Although we were poor, we grew up in a middle-class neighborhood. I never realized I didn't have what the neighbor kids had, but my older sister had a tougher time accepting that. Life was simple for me. I played outside, ran with the wind, flew kites, road bikes, and let my imagination take me on adventures.

Sunday Mass

Waking up on Sunday mornings in my home was the best. The smell of Grandma's Italian sauce was wonderful. The smells were so intoxicating, your taste buds danced for the main event. After breakfast, we attended mass. Later in the afternoon, family and friends came for dinner. That was our family tradition every Sunday without fail. We were very demonstrative with our affections and loud with our words, and we loved each other deeply.

On Saturday, everyone cleaned the house. The house rule was we could not go out to play until our chores were done and the house sparkled. Sometimes we'd take a ride in the car after our work was done. Mom, Grandma, my sister, brother, and I would all squeeze into our little Falcon and drive around, admiring people's homes. Life was good for the time being.

When I was around eight years old, something wonderful happened in our home. My older cousin, Carol, who always adored my mother, got engaged. While we were living with her family in New York, she promised my mother, "When I get married, I am going to move to California to be near you." First her fiancé, Jerry, came to live with us. He found a job and settled in with our family before their wedding. Having a man live with us brought a dynamic I never knew before. Grandma was happy. I'm sure she felt safe with a man in the home. I just loved him. We all loved Jerry. He brought joy and adventure into our lives. He was a happy guy who loved life. He was kind and loving to me. Once they were married, Carol joined Jerry here. Who knew that one day I would grow up to live with them?

My Father

When I was nine years old, my birth father came to see me. I was playing in our front yard, when a man drove up in a beautiful white Cadillac. My mother asked me, "Do you know who this man is?" I looked at her puzzled. She added, "It's your father." I thought, *My father? What does that mean?* I was never told anything about having a father. Now here's this stranger and I am supposed to simply accept him as my father? He took my sister and me out to lunch. He really didn't have much to say to me that I can remember, but I was only nine. My sister was fifteen, so he related better with her. She was so happy talking with him, and I was happy for them.

God's Touch

One Sunday morning while at mass with Grandma, I encountered my heavenly Father for the first time. I don't remember what holy day it was, but the service was so beautiful that it left an impression that stayed with me forever. I felt God's touch on me. I hungered so for a father's love, and I felt His presence all over me. From that day forward, I'd sneak off our block to go to confession and say my prayers in the church, in hopes I would feel Him again.

My Stepfather

When Mom met and married Ray, I finally had a good man in my life whom I thought would never leave us. Mom met Ray at the market where they worked. He was obviously smitten with her and would stop by after work with treats for all of us. It was quite obvious to him that we lived frugally, and there were many things that needed repair or replacement in our home. It wasn't long before his kindness and generosity became apparent. One day there was a knock on the door, and a delivery service brought new beds for all of us. I remember because, at the time, books were holding up my bed. We also received a delivery of all new appliances. Ray brought boxes of produce and other foods to our home. My grandmother was astonished. She probably thought she had died and gone to heaven. Once I blew up a balloon, and when it popped, the sound was so great it actually broke the TV screen. So guess what he bought us next? Right, a new television.

At ten years old, I was insecure and fearful but didn't know why. Perhaps it was because my grandmother had become sick.

In fifth grade, I received a terrible report card. All my friends were excited to show each other their grades, but I was embarrassed and humiliated. I ran all the way home and hid my report card under my grandmother's hospital bed. As frightened as I was, I knew God could help me. I sneaked out and ran all the way to church. I thought that if I confessed my sins and prayed, He would surely help me. The Catholic Church, with its unusual smells and light, comforted me. It seemed like the only place where I found peace outside my grandmother's arms. And because she was ill, I hadn't felt that touch for some time.

When I returned home, not only was I in trouble for leaving our street and going to church, but my little brother had found my report card. I was in big, big trouble. I had gone off without telling anyone, a grave offense in my house. Ray's methods of discipline were different from Grandma's. Raising and disciplining three stepchildren wasn't easy for him. He yelled and spanked because he and Mom feared something had happened to me. Although sick, Grandma still understood what was going on, and it upset her. She defended me and told them they should be happy I wanted to go to church. I felt scared and confused, but fear, not trust, dictated the tempo of our home.

My mother was an emotional wreck. The sadness associated

with Grandma's illness and the fear of her dying, along with working outside the home, raising three children and the heavy responsibilities that came with that, were too much for Mom. She didn't have the time or energy to comfort me. My young mind began to rationalize the events around me. I began to believe my family didn't love me, not that they were afraid something might have happened to me. I thought the teacher gave me poor grades because she hated me. What I didn't understand was she just wanted me to make better grades. I took everything personally. There was no one to explain, let alone help me with homework. I sought ways to help people so I could get their love. I did my sister's chores better than she did so I could please my mom and make her happy. In return, Mom gave me approval and affirmation. So that's how it worked; do things for people and, in return, be affirmed, accepted, and loved.

Death In The Family

The Bible say, **"Serve one another in love"** (Galatians 5:13 MSG). The Devil perverted my acts of service. I came to believe if I gave enough of myself, people would love and accept me, and God would be pleased. People-pleasing, fueled by fear of rejection, now directed my life. I wanted so badly to feel love and acceptance.

January 3, 1968. I remember it vividly. I was eleven years old, and Mom came home from the hospital. I could see she had been crying. She tried to speak to us kids but sobbed uncontrollably. When she finally spoke, her words totally changed my young life. My grandmother had died. I burst into tears and simply refused to believe it. *It's not true,* I thought. *Not my grandma. She would never leave me.* She had been a mother to me. She would never leave me without saying good-bye. Grandma had battled breast cancer, but I was never told this disease could end her life. I felt abandoned and couldn't accept that she was gone. For the next two weeks, I called the hospital day after day, asking to speak to my grandmother. They told me there was no one in the hospital with her name. Fear of abandonment and fear of death gained access to my confused and broken heart.

To make matters worse, my grandmother was laid to rest in New York. We didn't attend the funeral, because there wasn't any money to travel to New York. There was absolutely no closure for me.

My mother was extremely traumatized, and home would never be the same for any of us. My grandmother's death ravaged my soul. I was lost without her. At night I looked out my window and talked to the brightest star in the heavens as if it were my grandmother. She had more impact on me than anyone else in my life, and I thank my God for her investment in me. If it were not for her prayers and unconditional love for me, I probably wouldn't know Jesus today.

Keeping the promise they'd made to Grandma, Mom married Ray. After that, the dynamics of our home changed. My sister, Denise, didn't like that Mom had remarried. She got mixed up with a bad crowd and wanted no one telling her what to do. I'm sure she was hurting like the rest of us and didn't know how to cope with it. But her rebellion, already in full swing, intensified, causing relational problems between Mom and Ray. And what little peace I had known disappeared. The turmoil deepened Mom's depression. And Ray, whom I now called Pop, had no idea how to deal with any of it. As our lives spiraled down into hopelessness, the house we had rented for many years was sold. Leaving the home where we had lived and loved for so many years was one more loss we had to endure. When we moved, we left behind many fond memories.

Violations & Rebellion

By the time I began junior high school, I realized my life was different from my friends' lives. I couldn't go to the places they went or do what they did. After so many losses, Mom was consumed with the fear of losing her children. She needed to control every part of our lives to ensure we would be safe. She didn't realize her behavior had fostered my sister's rebellion and was now shaping my life. I could stay home or on my block with my girlfriend. *Period.* Those heavily enforced restrictions were like handcuffs. But I was now a teenager, and separation from my family and the desire to explore the world and who I was were in my nature. Try as they might, Mom and Pop didn't know their overprotection would push me right onto the same path of rebellion as my sister—only worse.

Because of my sister's rebellious behavior, my parents were overly strict with me. It drove me into anger and rejection of everything they said and wanted of me. All I wanted was to hang out with my friends. As I look back at that time, it seems that every Friday night I was grounded for something.

Sneaking Out and Getting Caught

When I was fourteen, I met Rick. He was very cute and understanding of me, but my parents forbade me from seeing him because his sister and my sister got in trouble together. But that didn't stop me. He filled a place in my heart left empty by the sorrow of my grandmother's death and made me feel alive. He gave me the attention my parents did not. I remember one night I snuck out to see Rick and got caught. That was a night forever etched in my memory because when I came home, I was faced with my stepfather's unspeakable and uncontrollable anger. He was waiting for me. That was the time that rage took hold of me. From that point on, I hated my parents. Pop had hurt me, and Mom didn't protect me. So, from then on rebellion became a way of life for me. Nothing and no one would or could stop me from doing whatever I wanted. I became fearless.

Because I could no longer live inside myself or in my home, I started running away. I'd run off and stay with friends for a week or so and then return home. My mother wouldn't know where I was. I felt so lonely. I ran through the streets at night, crying and screaming for God and my grandmother to help me. I was desperate. My pain was so overwhelming I wanted to die. The first time I tried to commit suicide, I was so depressed I took a handful of pills. During the early hours of the morning, I hallucinated. I saw spiders crawling in and out of me. I freaked out and awakened my mom. I said, "Look at them! Don't you see them?" She was beside herself because she saw nothing. When she rushed me to the doctor, he told her I was on drugs.

Being alone was impossible to endure. Through the years, I made several attempts to end my life, but thank God I was unsuccessful. I am reminded of Colossians 3:21 (CEV), "Parents, don't be hard on your children. If you are, they might give up."

Cursed

One of the times I ran away, I found out my birth father was looking for me and wanted me to call him. He told me if I lived with him, I would have more freedom. He seemed to understand me, so I told him everything about myself. I thought I could trust him, because he acted like my friend. I held back no secret. When he picked me up, I thought my life would be different. I started a new school and made friends. My stepmother moved out when she discovered I was moving in. And my father made sure I knew his marriage broke up because of me––not a good beginning for my new life. My father didn't take much interest in raising me. Because he performed in nightclubs in the evening, my paternal grandparents came during the day to take care of the necessities of the home. They stayed until my younger half-sister, Kristy, was in bed.

My father insisted I sleep with him. If I fell asleep on the couch, when he came in at three o'clock in the morning, he made me get up and climb into bed with him. I hated it, and my grandparents objected as well, but that didn't stop him. I thought it was weird, but I had no choice. Later in my life, he said he had insisted I sleep with him because he thought I would run away.

Living with my father was no better than living with Mom and Pop. I had no greater freedom or love from him. But one night, when two guys I knew from my old neighborhood phoned me that they wanted to stop by, he relented and allowed them. My dad called us into the family room. He told us, "I want you guys to hear something." I thought he was going to play his music for us, but instead, he played the recorded phone conversation I had with them earlier. The conversation was peppered with profanity, which he didn't like. I didn't know what to make of it, and it scared me.

He said, "I have something else to show you," and left the room.

He's Loading a Gun

One of my friends said, "He's loading a gun."

I said, "My dad is crazy but not *that* crazy."

He emerged from the bedroom and put the gun near my head. Then he said, "I don't know if you're —— my daughter. I really don't know who's —— her. But if she would let you talk to her with those words, who knows what she's done."

He said many other degrading things about me. Then he told them to get out and never show themselves on *his* block again. And if they did, he would shoot them.

Something happened to me that night that would affect all my relationships with men. My dad spiritually uncovered me and laid me out for the Devil to slaughter. I believe he set me up for rape and sexual abuse. He put a mark on me with his words. Words are powerful; they can chart the course of our lives and shape our future. **"Death and life are in the power of the tongue"** (Proverbs 18:21 NKJV).

That evening before he went to work, he had some young guy come over and stay with me so that I wouldn't run away. I slept on the couch while the stranger lay on the floor below me. I had to listen to him badmouth my mother, whom he had never met.

Back to Mom and Pop's

The next day, I told my mother what happened, and she came to get me. My six- weeks stay with my dad was over. I thought I would be safe, but when I arrived home, my dad called my stepfather and told him every dirty little secret I had confided to him. When Pop got off the phone, he slapped my face so hard it stunned me. And I was once again grounded.

A few weeks later, a girlfriend and I went to hang out at a guy's house. I'll call him "Tony." He was about three years older than me and over six feet tall. We started out in his garage with his brother and one of their friends, talking and listening to music. Tony invited me inside to "show me something." He took me into his bedroom and started kissing me. That was when he raped me. At first I was in shock. When I heard my girlfriend in the garage screaming as the two other guys raped her, I fought him and tried to get away. But at only five feet tall and weighing ninety-three pounds, I was no match for him. When they were done with us, Tony took us home, and my girlfriend and I never talked about it again. We never told anyone or reported it to the police. After that, my anger so dominated me that if someone looked at me wrong or gave me an attitude, I challenged him or her. I wasn't afraid to start fights if necessary. If no one would protect me, I would protect myself.

Not long after that, I was with some girlfriends getting gas for the car before going to a party. This guy pulled up on a motorcycle and looked at me. We said hi to each other. I didn't think much about it, and we went to the party. One of my girlfriends gave him my phone number without my knowledge, and he started calling me. He'd show up wherever I went. I wasn't interested in him at first, but he persisted and wore me down. I don't know how it happened, but I fell for him. I'll call him "Bill." Bill became very possessive of me, and I thought that showed he loved me. If someone just looked at me, Bill was on a mission to hurt him. It felt good that he was looking out for me. But sometimes he'd get rough with me. After fighting, the passion of making up felt like love to me. People who loved each other hurt each other. According to my experience, that's how life worked. He and I even talked about marriage. The sad thing is, we both were so broken and codependent, we didn't know what a healthy relationship looked like.

Helicopters and Police Cars

At the end of our relationship, I got angry with Bill and decided to break up with him. I had my mom take everything he ever gave me back to him. I wanted to punish him. When she gave him his stuff, he went crazy. He threw them at her, got into his car, and took off. Mom followed him as he drove like a maniac to my house. He lost a tire off his car, but that didn't slow him down. He drove all the way with sparks flying from the axle as it scraped the road. Scared to death and not knowing what he was capable of, my mom called the police. Helicopters and police cars were at my house immediately, and he was arrested. As they took him away, he cried and swore how much he loved and needed me.

Bill called me from the county jail the next morning. My mom insisted I tell him I never wanted to see him again. I had to do as she said, but I wanted him more than anything. Because I was fifteen and he was twenty-one, my parents would do whatever it took to keep us apart. He became enraged because he didn't think I wanted him anymore. He threatened to make public some inappropriate photos I had let him take. My mom was listening to our conversation, and she flipped out. She threatened to have him charged with statutory rape, but that only made him more determined. Not liking to be threatened, he called an ex-girlfriend to get those pictures out of his house. When I went to school the next day, the photos were being passed around for everyone to see. I was so ashamed and heartbroken, yet I still wanted that man. I wanted what passed for love from him. That's when I quit school.

Because I was on probation for running away, I was forbidden by the state of California and my parents to have any communication with Bill. If I wrote to him, my letters would be intercepted. My parents let me move in with my sister, Denise, and her family. This didn't last long. She accused me of being with her husband, so I moved out, lied about my age, and got my own apartment.

Feelings of loneliness and abandonment invaded my life, so I started seeing someone else. I didn't want to be alone. The one I thought I loved was in jail but had taken up with his old girlfriend to hurt me. After a few months, Bill was released, and I couldn't wait to see him again. He came to my apartment. He acted as though he cared, but his true intention was to make me pay for everything that had happened to him. In order for us to be together, he suggested I turn myself in to the police, try to get emancipated, or live with another family. I believed he loved me, so I turned myself in and told the police I didn't want to go home. When my mom showed up for court, she asked to see me. I told her to leave and that I wanted nothing to do with her. I was angry with my parents and blamed them for everything that went wrong with my boyfriend. I couldn't see that I had any part in it.

Locked up at L.A. County Jail

After twenty-four hours of being locked up in LA County Juvenile Hall and being told what to do, I'd had enough. I wanted out. My probation officer was working on having me placed in Malibu, where there was a home with horses, but there was no room just yet. He was a Christian man, who had come to care about me and knew the path I was on was self-destructive. That would be another part of the plan from my heavenly Father. I always cried out to Him for help. I just didn't know He really listened. **"For My thoughts are not your thoughts, nor are your ways, My ways, declares the Lord"** (Isaiah 55:8 ISV).

I was now a ward of the court, and my mother had lost all parental rights. While I was in juvenile hall, my cousin Carol wrote me a beautiful letter about how she believed in me and that there wasn't anything I couldn't do if I just tried. Carol's mother came to see me. I was no longer the innocent girl she once knew. She saw I was in serious trouble, and it saddened her. Within days, I was released and on a plane to Boston with my aunt and uncle to start a new life.

I moved in with Carol and Jerry, and they laid out new rules and structure. I attended a vocational trade school, where I studied cosmetology. It was challenging, going to school and following the rules, but I was grateful I was no longer locked up. I made friends quickly and got a job after school, assisting at a hair salon. To help me deal with the sadness and anger, I attended therapy sessions every week for the next three years. I experienced my first level of healing through that therapy. My family loved me unconditionally. I should have been completely happy, but I was plagued by this nagging feeling that California was better. I had to get back there because I still wanted my old boyfriend and the life of partying.

On my eighteenth birthday, I was no longer a ward of the court, so I decided to return to California. I arranged to see Bill. As soon as I saw him, I thought, *This is what I have been crying over for three years?* I was in utter disbelief! He no longer had an emotional hold on me. He returned the offensive photos to me, and I burned them. But I still felt so much shame. When summer ended, I returned to the East Coast to work full time in the salon.

Pursued by God

A year passed, and I bounced back to California again. After attempting to live with my parents, I moved into an apartment with a friend. It was not to be a safe place for me. I began seeing a guy who had gone to high school with my sister. He had pursued me through the years, but at the time, I only liked him as a friend. I gave the relationship a shot but knew it wouldn't work, because we were very different. After an argument on the phone, I told him I was done. Shortly after I hung up, he showed up at my apartment in a rage. He pounded on the door and forced his way inside. He abused me physically and verbally. He raped me and left me there like a piece of trash. It seemed like I had a sign on my forehead that read, "Please have your way with me." I cried out to God once again. That afternoon, I walked to the corner to buy cigarettes. I was still crying. A young man approached me and asked if he could pray for me. He tried to encourage me and invited me to his church.

That same week, an old friend, Rick, came looking for me to tell me Jesus had appeared to him. He shared with me all the wonderful things he had experienced with Christ. He was now on a mission to see all his friends were saved. I am so thankful for the boldness he had. I believe God used him to direct me to the cross. He continued sending people into my life to direct me to Him, my heavenly Father, and receive the true healing I needed. I just didn't know it yet. I often wonder how Rick's life has turned out. I pray God is a very close presence in his life today. God bless you, Rick!

My Future Husband

One Sunday afternoon at the park, where my friends met each week, I saw Randy—the man who would become my husband. I had known Randy for a long time but hadn't seen him for three years. We talked and shared what had been going on in our lives. He had just finished his service in the marines. I told him I had just moved back from Massachusetts. He started calling me, wanting to see me, but he was just a friend to me. When he asked me to go camping over the weekend, I turned him down because I wasn't ready for a boyfriend. I was suffering from the recent abuse and rape, and I wasn't ready for another relationship.

Over the next few months, I often saw him at parties. Finally, I decided we could start dating. He was different from all the crazy guys I had dated. When my sister invited me to her church, Randy went with me. It was like no church we'd been in before. Many of the people looked like bikers. They wore vests that announced they were "Soldiers for Christ." I was shocked to see people raising their hands and worshipping Jesus. I thought they were crazy. My brother-in-law, Rick, had his eyes closed, and I saw peace all over him. Something was different here.

I've Been Praying For You!

At the end of the service, a guy ran across the room toward me with a huge smile on his face. It was the young man I had met on the street the day I was raped. He said, "It's so good to see you. I've been praying for you!" Sadly, that night would be the last time I ever saw him. Seeing him that night was one of those divine appointments from God. I know one day we will see each other in heaven.

God heard my cry that day. He lifted me out of a pit, up out of the miry clay, and set my feet upon the Rock. I would like to say I started going to church regularly then, but I didn't. I wanted the Lord badly, but I never knew I could have a personnel relationship with Him. The Spirit was wooing me, but I wasn't ready to give up my sin.

Randy and I began attending a Wednesday night Bible study. Every week we'd go to the Bible study, and I would ask Jesus into my heart. But I never *felt* saved.

Deborah and Randy Parker on their Wedding Day

In 1977 Randy and I were married. But there was no peace for me. Fear of death haunted my soul. I was afraid that, now I had found love, I would get a call he had died, and I would be alone and unloved once again. I was in bondage to the same things that tormented my mother. Feelings of insecurities overshadowed me. I put pressure on Randy, demanding he prove he was committed to the relationship and that he wouldn't cheat on me. When I became pregnant for the first time, I was sick in bed for most of the nine months. Randy was immature and still wanted to spend time with his friends, hang out, go fishing. I was pregnant and miserable, and all I wanted was for him to spend time with me. And it wasn't happening for me.

One afternoon when I was home alone, there was a knock at

my door. Without a second thought, I opened it, and there stood the man who raped me when I was fifteen. He'd come to see Randy about something. Numbed with disbelief, I let him in. He acted as though nothing had ever happened between us. I felt sick to my stomach, and all the shame and intimidation from the past rose up in me. When Randy came home, I went to our bedroom. I sat there stunned that I allowed this rapist into my home. Why had I done that?

Life Redeemed

My husband wasn't able to make me feel loved and needed. I served him, but I got very little in return. Although we both were relationally handicapped, I was very demonstrative of my affection, while he was unable and unwilling to show emotions. He was not good at sharing his love and devotion to me, let alone any feelings.

The only way I could get Randy to show me any emotion, to show me he cared, was if we had an argument. He then had to prove to me by his words and actions that he loved me. I'd make him feel so badly he'd cry.

Starting Our Family

In July 1978, our beautiful daughter, Danielle, was born. I felt it was my greatest accomplishment. *Danielle needed me.* I never felt so happy and complete in my life. I was a devoted mother. If she made a sound, I was there. She was the most beautiful child I'd ever seen, and I couldn't believe I was her mother.

In the midst of mayhem and chaos, sometimes there's a glimpse of truth. One night Randy and I got into a terrible argument. Our words were particularly abusive and ugly. In the middle of it, Randy picked up our family Bible (we hadn't yet begun to read it) and declared the only way to get our marriage to work was in this book. He was right, but it would be four more years before we came to have a personal relationship with Jesus.

In February of 1982, our beautiful son, Wesley, was born. We had a daughter and now a son. Life was good; our family was complete.

A couple of months after Wesley's birth, a girlfriend invited me to West Valley Christian Church. The kids and I started attending there, and I loved it. Every Sunday this church had an altar call. I felt this strong pull to go forward and give my life to Jesus. For a long time I resisted because I would then have to say the Sinner's Prayer and be baptized. Doing that felt like a betrayal to my Catholic family.

The Presence of God

One Sunday morning I felt the presence of God strongly calling me forward to give my life to Him. A battle went on within me, until I could no longer resist the Holy Spirit. I surrendered. On the day of my baptism, I stepped into the water and an overwhelming feeling enveloped me––*pure love*. I experienced a dramatic deliverance. That day I truly participated with Him in his death, burial, and resurrection. As I sank beneath the waters, it proclaimed death to my past, the burial of all that was behind me, and the resurrection of a new life for me in *Him*. I met Jesus. He revealed himself to me. I had never felt a love or acceptance like this. Forever changed, redeemed by His death, I was washed and cleansed by His redeeming love. Praise you, Jesus, for dying and cleansing me with your precious blood.

"He walked with me and talked with me," all the day long. The words of that hymn soon became a declaration to my soul. I dove right into the Word of God. I wanted to know everything about Jesus. Not long after that, Randy gave his life to Jesus as well. His commitment to the Lord was different than mine. I wanted Jesus and all He had for me and my family. I plunged into the Word of God as I had into the waters of baptism. Randy, on the other hand, was more casual about his pursuit of the Lord. He still wanted to play baseball and hang out with his friends. Our life wasn't perfect, but we had new hope.

Fear and Panic Attacks

Even though my life with Jesus was glorious, my marriage still suffered. When we argued, his words often triggered the fear and pain from all my sexual abuse. I felt dirty, unloved, and ashamed. Considering divorce, I scheduled an appointment with my pastor. As I began to share, I started to cry uncontrollably. My eyes started twitching, and my hands started to curl and become distorted. That had never happened to me before. Tormenting fear engulfed me. Pastor Glenn sat next to me, patted me on my back, and spoke words of comfort. He reassured me everything was going to be all right. I thought, *I have now become insane, and I will lose my children forever.* They were the only things in this world that really matter to me, outside of Jesus. I feared someone would take, kill, rape, or molest my kids, and their lives would end up as mine. They would never survive. While I appreciated Pastor's comfort, I knew I was in trouble, and fear was becoming an idol in my life. This was just the beginning of the panic attacks. Fear consumed every part of me.

I experienced my next panic attack while sitting in a financial health seminar with my husband. Suddenly, I couldn't breathe; I thought I was dying. Randy was no help. I went outside for air, but that didn't help me. I went into the bathroom and wet my face and neck with water. But my heart still raced, and my lungs tightened. So I went back inside and told Randy he needed to take me to the nearest hospital. After that incident, I didn't want to leave my home. I'd only go to places I absolutely had to go. Fear was winning.

Besides, I didn't need to go out. I had all that fulfilled me at home ... my children. Danielle was beautiful, precious, sweet, and always compliant, no matter what might be asked of her. She always listened and was a loving big sister, always looking out for her little brother. Wesley was a handsome little boy with a huge smile and a sparkle in his eyes. He would look at me and melt my heart. There was a mischievous side to him as well, but he had conviction in his little heart. If he did something wrong I would find him on the timeout chair, where he put himself. Very affectionate then and now, he was my love bug, always having to be near me, making some sort of body contact. Wherever we went he always made a new friend.

My son's sense of adventure and mischief were complicated by his being hyperactive. I was constantly running on a frequency of terror because of the predicaments I would find him in. Every gray hair on my head got there because of him. He had several brushes with death, both as a child and an adult. But praise Jesus, He protected him and carried him through.

Wesley — A Call on His Life

Wesley has a call on his life. I know this because God whispered it to me when Wesley was a young boy. In his preteens, he began to receive prophetic words from leaders in the church. They told him he was called by God, who had a plan for his life. That plan and calling was for him to be a pastor. He received so many prophetic words at one time it troubled him. He wanted to be a baseball player. He often said, "When I am thirty-eight, I will answer the call on my life."

Despite the fact God had called him, I still worried. Every morning before school, we went through a ritual of putting on the armor of God. I would pray over my son and daughter, drop them off, and then drive around the school, praying God would send His angels to guard them.

One morning after dropping my son off at school, the Lord asked me what I was afraid of. I told Him I was afraid for their lives. He said, "If I pulled you out of the mire, what makes you think I can't do that for your son?" At that point I knew I couldn't protect my son from going through difficulties in his life.

The way I disciplined my son was not always in his best interest. I disciplined out of frustration and anger. Wesley wasn't the kind of child you could tell not do something because he could get hurt. He was fearless and reckless, which scared me to no end. I sometimes disciplined him with a heavy hand. I manipulated him with the Word of God, thinking it would knock some sense into him. I would tell him Jesus wasn't happy with him because of what he'd just done. As soon as the words left my lips, I'd hear the Lord. "I did not say that. You tell him that I didn't say that, and ask him for forgiveness." Convicted and cut to the heart, I did as Jesus told me. I wanted all the best things for my son, but I drove him away because of my fear and control.

Ministry

As we grew in our walk with the Lord, we met other Christians. One of them invited us to the Church on the Way in Van Nuys, for a Christmas performance in 1986. We enjoyed the fellowship and teaching so much, we soon became members. Sitting under Pastor Jack's teaching was wonderful and liberating. I felt I had gone on to graduate school. His love for the Lord and his depth in the delivery of the Word brought me deeper into the knowledge of Jesus. I am thankful to my heavenly Father that He made Pastor Jack Hayford my spiritual father.

Wanting to grow in my understanding of spiritual gifts, I attended a Bible study with a group of woman. I began a discipline of spending time alone with the Holy Spirit, and He revealed Himself to me in a way I never knew was possible. His glory is life changing. I began to comprehend the dynamic of the Holy Spirit. Jesus said He would send the Comforter, the Holy Spirit to guide and teach us and lead us into all truths (John 16:13 GNB). Those truths became a reality for me in orchestrating healing and deliverance in my life as well as in the lives of others.

That ministry began around the time I started an after-school Bible study for my daughter and her girlfriends. From time to time, the girls and I planned events for them. One Friday night, the mother of one of the girls was having a bout with fear. She struggled to let her daughter attend the event we had planned. I assured her I would take good care of her daughter. I asked the woman if I could pray for her to receive the baptism of the Holy Spirit. As soon as I laid my hands on her, she began to growl, and it looked like her jaw was dislocated. I wasn't afraid, and I kept on praying for her until the growling stopped. She looked at me, surprised, and asked, "What just happened?" I told her something bad had to leave in order for her to know truth.

Demons and Deliverance

The next morning, I called a precious sister in the Lord and told her what had happened. She said it sounded like deliverance. I asked what that meant, and she said a demon had left the woman. I was now very curious to know where this demon had gone and asked her if it was now in my home. She chuckled. "No. It goes to a dry place." This began a season in my life when whomever I would pray for experienced some type of healing or deliverance.

A leader in our church encouraged Randy and me to attend a Cleansing Stream seminar. This ministry was fairly new to the church, and we were eager to see what it was about. Cleansing Stream was the vehicle God used to bring healing and deliverance to us both. Before the seminar was over, we signed up for the next one. We were starving for all God had for our lives. During that season, the Lord brought trust, love, and reconciliation into our marriage. We received healing from our past, new purpose for our marriage, and we began to serve Jesus as one.

Eventually, we became part of the leadership for this ministry and served the body of Christ for many years. As part of the accountability within the ministry, it was required that we be in a process whereby God could continue to restore our souls, our lives.

We took our role as parents seriously. Our family did everything together, including church two to three times a week. My husband and I taught our children the Word and covered them in prayer. I wanted the Lord to fully govern the courses of their lives. We didn't want them to go through the difficulties we had experienced. We taught them the importance of obedience to the Lord and walking in holiness in order for His peace and blessing to rest on and dwell in them. I never expected them to do anything I wasn't willing to do. I lived what I taught, striving to reflect Christ in my life. I was careful about everything and everybody that came into my home, and I didn't allow movies, music, or friends I thought could be a hindrance to them. But with control and fear ruling my life, I had many challenges to overcome.

It wouldn't be long before Danielle served in the Cleansing Stream ministry as well. From time to time, she traveled with us to seminars around the country, ministering in healing and deliverance. She also served as part of the worship team, ushering in the presence of God. Danielle's life portrayed innocence, purity, and pure beauty. She walked with so much wisdom and reflected godly character wherever she went. Danielle loved Jesus with all her heart and wanted to please Him as well as us.

Prelude to Disaster

At this time, Danielle worked for a Christian record label and became part of a team called 'Nitro Praise,' with whom she performed at churches and Christian conferences throughout the United States. That's where she met her first husband. He was an artist signed to the record label, as well as a youth pastor.

He pursued our daughter, and as difficult as it was for Randy and me, we allowed it. He was a Christian and a pastor, so we thought he would be a gentleman with her. He wanted to propose to her right away, but Randy said no. We felt the relationship was moving too quickly.

As our children were growing up, I always prayed for their spouses. We wanted them to marry the person God had for them. Randy and I also felt strongly that whoever married our daughter needed to know the responsibility of his headship in the home. We weren't willing to give her to any believer who came along, no matter how good he looked to the church or to the world. Our daughter was a precious gift from God. He entrusted us with her life, and we knew we would one day answer to Him for our role as her parents.

While I knew with every fiber of my being that he wasn't right for her, I had no hard evidence. Was I guilty of judging one of

God's kids? My husband and I worried that all those red flags we saw were the result of unrealistic expectations on our part. I shared my concerns and feelings with church leaders, and we diligently prayed about it. But I came away feeling condemned for being too critical of this young man.

Randy and I doubted ourselves and second-guessed our discernment. And after all, he did everything we asked of him, including completing his education, going through the Cleansing seminar, and submitting to Randy's mentorship on how to be the head of his family.

We continually pushed back the wedding date until the pastor of the church they attended told them they needed to stick with their date and get married.

Danielle's Wedding

So the wedding was on. Before the ceremony, I asked her for the last time, "Is he who you want to marry?" She said yes. My lovely daughter thought as I did, that she was being too critical of him and that, although she didn't love this man, in time she would grow to love him.

Walking down the aisle that day was agonizing for me. I remember one of my friends saying to me, "Smile. This is supposed to be a happy day." But it wasn't. It felt so very wrong.

As part of the ceremony, Randy prayed over the newlyweds and passed the mantle of our spiritual covering for our daughter over to her husband. From deep within my soul, I felt something leave, and tears stung my eyes. *What have we done?* I wondered. The emptiness left behind seemed like a nightmare playing out before my eyes.

Danielle married this man knowing he wasn't the one God had for her. When she finally confided to me that she had felt the same way as I did, I groaned deep within my spirit. I was grieved and heart broken. Everybody went along with this marriage despite our misgivings. We convinced ourselves that we were wrong, church leadership was right, and we were just being too critical of him.

I suspect that Danielle consented to the marriage because of the control she felt from me. For whatever reasons, it was done, and there wasn't a thing I could do. I felt so sick that I had given her to someone who didn't deserve her and wasn't right for her, either.

Broken

Just as soon as they were married, it happened. That bad feeling I was having and getting prayer for hit me full force. I had a complete nervous breakdown. My husband found me lying on our daughter's bedroom floor, where I had been crying for hours. If I wasn't crying, I sat in a chair, staring into space, thinking of what had happened. Thirteen hours flew by like it was an hour to me. For the next few weeks, I took everyone on an emotional roller coaster. One minute I'd be crying, and the next I'd be screaming at everyone. My perfect little family was not perfect anymore.

Around three o'clock one morning, unable to sleep due to tormenting thoughts, I grabbed all the money I could find in the house, took Randy's keys, and jumped into his truck. Because I felt no one understood the pain I was in or how to help me, I left. I decided to drive north, up the coast. I stopped at Morro Bay and got a hotel room. That afternoon I walked out to the rock. That was where the Lord spoke to me. He told me to write down all the emotions I had about everything. Then He instructed me to gather a number of smooth stones. That night in my hotel room, He told me to write each emotion on one of the rocks I had gathered earlier.

The next morning, following God's instructions, I returned to Morro Rock. God led me to sit on the jetty. I was hesitant to sit because many little animals crawled in and out of the large rocks. He said, "Don't be afraid. They won't bother you." I sat down. On my right I noticed the rocks were many different sizes. God said, "Your heart has been broken. It is fragmented from all the hurt you have had in your life." He told me the rocks represented each individual hurt, some greater than others. I noticed again the animals crawling through the rocks. God said the creatures were like the enemy of my soul that rubbed against all the raw, broken places of my heart. The Enemy was using my brokenness, hurt, and pain to destroy me. I cried in utter despair.

Then He drew my attention to my left. "These rocks represent people in your life. Some people have hurt you more than others." The rock directly in front of me was the largest. God said, "That rock represents your daughter." I looked more closely and noticed affixed to the rock an eye hook large enough to moor a dinghy. "I have unhooked her from you, and that's why you are feeling this pain." I sobbed uncontrollably as my mind was flooded with thoughts of betrayal. My heavenly Father uprooted my false security of what I thought love was. I was raw and vulnerable. My thought process became a whipping post to the open wounds of my soul. It left me in an unbearable state of being. I wanted to die.

Idols

As I sat there in agony, trying to process it all, I realized my children had become idols in my life. They were the very center of our home. All the fears from my past once again made me believe I was unlovable. No one would invest in my emotions as I did for them.

Atop Morro Rock sat a large bird of prey. It looked to me like an eagle. I watched the bird leave the rock, swoop around, and return to its original spot. The Lord said, "You are like the rock, and I am the eagle. It may look like I'm leaving, but I'm not. I will never leave you, because I dwell in you."

Then the Lord told me to go out to the edge of the jetty. "Take the stones and paper from the night before," He said. "Make an altar for Me with the rocks. Place on top the paper you have written and burn it." I did as He said, weeping the whole time. When He spoke to me next, His words were full of love. He said He'd been waiting for me, and He knew from the foundations of the earth we would meet here on this day.

As I prepared to leave, I asked Him if there was something there I could take to remind me of this day. I looked down and noticed among all the huge rocks, a tiny one, half the size of my thumb. It was bright white, with a corner cut off. The inside was completely black. He said, "This is how the church looks––clean on the outside but broken and dark on the inside." I also found a small piece of green glass made very smooth by the pounding of the ocean. He told me that green stands for life, and I was to choose life.

I drove down to San Simeon to walk on the beach. I discovered a sand dollar alone on the wide expanse of sand. I remembered there were little bones inside that looked like doves, and although I wanted to see them, I didn't want to break it open. I knew He would reveal to me, when the time was right, the significance of that sand dollar.

The next day I checked out of my hotel. I couldn't extend my stay, because they were booked; it was Fourth of July weekend. I asked her if she knew of any other vacancies nearby. She told me no and not to go north, because they would be booked for the holiday. I would have better luck going south. That meant I would be headed toward home, something I did not want to do. I set out looking for other places to stay. I found a very seedy motel. I checked in but then decided I didn't want to stay.

I discovered while getting gas that Randy had canceled my credit cards. I was so furious with him. I did not want to go home, to a place where I felt unloved and misunderstood.

Little Doves

Near Santa Maria, I noticed a flea market. Don't ask me why I stopped, but I did. As I walked around, I came across a booth selling only sand dollars. There were thousands of them. Several lay open, revealing five "little doves." I immediately knew what God was saying. *Five means grace.* I left and headed toward home, crying and begging Him to help me. He said, "You are going to get through this by My grace." I thought, *Your grace? I'm dying inside. Why haven't You removed this tormenting pain? All You would have to do is speak a word, and it would be done.*

The Lord wanted me to confront my fears and die to them. I was still wrestling with going home; I did not want to face everything I had run from. There was an inner struggle going on so deep that I had a vision of me cutting myself and pulling off my skin. It was so demonic. I envisioned myself in a deep hole, and I couldn't climb out. My pain was so deep, so great. I began to understand why people hurt themselves physically—to mask the pain they feel on the inside.

That afternoon, I returned home to face everything I had run from. My daughter was there. and when she saw me, she looked scared, made a phone call, and left. I would like to say the emotional pain only lasted a few weeks, but it didn't. I never imagined one could feel such hopelessness and despair. I had not one ounce of hope or desire for any future. My life was done.

On the flip side were my family's emotions. My husband tried to love me the best he knew how and to protect our children from my crazy behavior. Randy tried to be sensitive toward me. I never noticed the pain he might have felt; I was consumed with my own pain. My husband is a wonderful man, who desired to see God heal and restore his family, especially his wife. As for my children, they had no idea what I was going through. They were extremely confused and very hurt. They had never seen that side of me before.

New Life

Rejection and abandonment got a foothold in my soul at an early age, causing me to feel afraid, insecure, and unloved. I had suffered from sadness and fear of death. My physical and sexual abuse left me feeling unwanted, unloved, and depressed. Fear of not being loved caused me to become performance driven, longing for acceptance not only from humankind but from God. If I wasn't accepted, fear told me no one cared for me, deepening my insecurities and self-doubt. I suffered from disappointment, loneliness, and sadness. The spirit of the "fear of death" linked up with control to create an environment where I could feel safe. But I never felt safe, no matter how hard I tried to control things. I was terrified something bad would happen to my kids, and it forced me to attempt to control every aspect of their lives.

Children are very compliant when they're young, but as they mature, they begin to think for themselves. Therefore, the struggle between us intensified. I feared losing them forever. The Devil had woven a web of deception over my life. In turn, I brought a lot of hurt to my family.

With the advent of panic attacks, I felt I was losing complete control of myself and of life around me. Even though I was a believer, the Devil had come to steal, kill, and destroy. But there's a verse in the Bible that promises what the Enemy meant for evil, God will use for good (Genesis 50:20 GNB).

Unfailing Love

At this point, I began a long season of facing all my fears. I was unable to do anything on my part for freedom. All I once did for that freedom no longer worked. He told me I had put Him in a box. The one thing I could do was surrender all to Him and die to myself.

Five years later, in the midst of continuous trials, my son became a father at age twenty. When I found out we were going to have a granddaughter, I created a nursery awaiting her arrival. When Juliana was born, she captured all our hearts. I knew God was going to use her for my healing, and it was love at first sight.

It would be one year after Juliana's birth that my mother and sister were diagnosed with cancer, within two months of each other. Once again my faith was tried. Over the next five years, my aunt (Carol's mother), mother, nephew, grandmother, and uncle would die. I literally went through hell! So much death surrounded our family. The Lord made me face each trial and tragedy one at a time. It brought me face-to-face with my fear of death and deep-seated insecurity. It felt as though I was being sliced open with each loss. I was emotionally dead, stinking dead, and I wondered how much more I would have to die. I had nothing left, nothing to give.

Everything I loved, everything of importance to me, seemed to have faded away. First my daughter, and then through death, my closest relatives were taken from me. I loved ministering to God's people, but even that desire was gone. I loved serving in the church, but that was taken from me as well. Even my foundation in Jesus was removed. Though I loved Him with all my heart, it was based out of fear, performance, and false ideology. I didn't know who I was or what I believed about anything. All I once knew lay shattered at my feet.

My son Wesley and daughter Juliana

Juliana's mother was going through many struggles in her own life. She already had a two-year-old son by another man. Wesley was very concerned about the environment for his daughter to be raised in. He thought, as we did, that it would be in Juliana's best interest for her to come and live with him at our home. She truly is a gift from my heavenly Father. The day she was born, God smiled on our family. I wish I had let God use Wesley's new fatherhood to change him and bring him into manhood, but I didn't. Once again, there was a battle. But God gave Randy and I the privilege of raising this little angel from birth.

My little Juliana is already a deeply devoted young Christian girl. She loves Jesus with her whole heart. She is very passionate about her walk with Him. In fact, she is my little warrior princess. We are to enter into the kingdom with childlike faith, much like Juliana. Even at this tender age of eleven, she is ready and prepared as His betrothed and beloved bride. She is a beautiful reflection of Jesus Christ and an inspiration to all who meet her. I love you, Jules!

Wesley's Conversion

Juliana's dad, Wesley, finally committed his life to Jesus in 2012. Although God is still working on my son's future, it is well with my soul. I have finally learned to surrender him to Jesus and trust He will carry him through to fulfill his destiny in Him. **"I know the plans that I have for you, declares the Lord. They are plans for peace and not disaster plans to give you a future filled with hope"** (Jeremiah 29:11 GW). That hope is Jesus.

Although life has been tough, I am grateful for my life's experiences and how I've grown, I am still being refined. I thank my God that every challenge and obstacle that stood in my path, He was there to see me through. He used those things to make me stronger, learn to trust, and draw me closer to Him. As I yielded my life to Him many times in worship, I surrendered all of me for all of Him. God is patient and long suffering with us all. He waited for me to surrender completely, so He could walk me through His redemption. He's not interested in how I "do" church or what I can do for Him. However, He is eager for me to understand that He loves me, and His grace is sufficient for me.

I never understood His unfailing love for me. It reaches to the deepest places that are hidden in secret. His Spirit sought me in the midnight hour, anticipating my surrender. All that consumed me once had consumed Him. He bore it all on the cross past, present, and future. God wiped out the charges that were against us for disobeying the law of Moses. He took them away and nailed them to the cross (Colossians 2:14 CEV). Jesus paid it in full.

Nothing I could do would merit what was freely given. He watches and waits so patiently for a surrendered heart. Can I trust Him? I would have to say with my whole heart, yes! He knew exactly what happened to me in my life better than I knew myself. If I were the only one He ever created, He still would've died just for me. That's amazing love!

Walking by Faith

If we are willing to follow His still small voice, walk by faith, not give in to doubt and unbelief, and trust Him with our future, we can abide in His peace. He is pure love, forever faithful, all-knowing, all-consuming, and all-powerful. When He thinks the time is right, He executes judgment on the enemy of our souls. He walks us through our trials so that we can conquer the giants in our lives. Face your fears, understand your struggles, and lay them on the altar for Christ to burn them up. Yes, it's death, but to a false identity. My identity is supposed to be in Him. His thoughts and motives are pure. But most of all, He is the lover of my soul.

Jesus wants to renew our mind and direct our thoughts (Philippians 4:8 CEV). Finally, my friends, keep your minds on whatever is true, pure, right, holy, friendly, and proper. Don't ever stop thinking about what is truly worthwhile and worthy of praise. It is time to stand up, take back our God-given authority, and shine; shine like the Son. Christ is in you, the hope of glory.

Let us, then, hold firmly to the faith we profess. For we have a great High Priest who has gone into the very presence of God—Jesus, the Son of God. (Hebrews 4:14 GNB)

Our High Priest is not one who cannot feel sympathy for our weaknesses. On the contrary, we have a High Priest who was tempted in every way that we are, but did not sin. (Hebrews 4:15)

Let us have confidence, then, and approach God's throne,

where there is grace. There we will receive mercy and find grace to help us just when we need it. (Hebrews 4:16)

I want to thank my heavenly Father for His great love, faithfulness, and the resurrection power of the cross. My husband, Randy, of thirty-six years of marriage, no matter how bad it got, you believed in me and never gave up. My children Danielle, Wesley, and Juliana with all my heart, my desire is to see you walk in your God-given destiny be healed and prosper in all things. I love you all so much!

And finally, thanks to Patricia Little, a gifted writer and sister in Christ, who helped me edit my chapter and capture the very essence of my story. Thank you, thank you, thank you.

Contact information:
Deborah Parker
P.O. Box 4602
West Hills CA 91308
deborahparker357@gmail.com

Barbara Allen

"Before I formed you in the womb I knew you, before you were born, I set you apart;"
Jeremiah 1:5 (New International Version)

"We've only Just Begun" (The Carpenters)

I was born to sing. I can't imagine not singing, and I can't remember a time when I wasn't singing. My journey has been defined by music, all sorts of music. Pop, ballad, gospel, disco, classical, jazz, opera, and traditional and contemporary Christian music have all planted seeds in my soul. And it all began in the '60s.

"Doh … a … dee, a … fee … may … dee. Reh … a … dro … o … gol … duh … suh." The disconnected melody and almost unidentifiable lyrics broke the stillness of early morning as Olive and Ken Sharp lay in bed, listening. I was little more than a toddler, barely two years old so the story goes, but I was standing in my crib and singing in quiet, broken phrases, "Meh … a … nay … I … caw … ma … se."

"Listen," my mom said, "it's do a deer." *The Sound of Music* was the hit of the moment, and its catchy tunes were played regularly on the radio. The two of them listened, surprised and amused that their little girl had not only memorized the words but also managed to impart a recognizable tune. It had begun—my love affair with singing!

I was born the youngest of three children (my older

sister, Joy, and brother, Kevin, had the lead on me by nine years and four and a half years, respectively). By all accounts, I was a "surprise," whatever that may mean! Whether it was a surprise how I was conceived or just a surprise when I actually appeared, I'm not sure, but I was here and determined to be heard!

Precocious from early in life, I was enamored of all things singing and dancing. I remember sitting on my dad's shoulders as he danced with me in front of a huge mirror we had in front of the fireplace. "Can you dance the 'Merry Widow Waltz' with me?" I could ... and I did regularly! I was definitely a daddy's girl; actually, I still am! Dad had nicknames for all of us. Joy was Joy-eva-ova, mimicking the way she said her own name, Joy Heather Olive, when she was a baby. Kevin was Konkin' the Mate. I have no idea where that came from. I was "Tooby was and is and are and grand, the best little girlie in the land," or just "Tooby" for short.

Born into a loving, Christian family in the northwest of England, my early years were shaped by going to church on a Sunday and being very involved in the children's music there. My dad was the children's choir director, though the first one to admit he had no training or knowledge of vocal pedagogy! My mom was a pianist, who played for the children's and adults' choirs. In fact, it was her playing of the organ and "peeking" over the top of the music stand that first caught my dad's eye in the congregation. Why he wasn't listening to the sermon I don't know, but for him at least, it was love at first sight. For her, he was a very handsome, slightly Norwegian looking, white blonde-haired stranger who had the audacity to stare at her throughout the service. What girl could resist that? They married!

In those days, my mom played what was commonly called a "pedal organ," which ran on compressed air. To get sound out of it, you had to continually depress two foot pedals while playing the keys. It worked a little like an accordion. We often laughed that if it only had a steering wheel, we could all get on it and drive to church! Sometimes Mom brought the organ home from church so she could practice. When she finished playing, I hopped right on it and entertained myself for hours. I loved that! Mom also had a wonderful ability to harmonize any tune with her resonant alto voice. Dad was less inclined to want to perform, but he had, and still does have, a great appreciation and love of classical music. To this day, whenever it's the "Last Night of the Proms" broadcast from the Royal Albert Hall, London, you will find him glued to the television and often helping the conductor stay on track by waving his arms around. I guess you could say I came from a musical family.

Severe Asthma Attacks

When I was just a few months old, I was diagnosed with asthma. Every now and then, I had a severe asthma attack that left my parents greatly concerned. This was in the days before medication to control asthma was available, so I relied on medication that was administered during an attack to help stabilize me. Between the ages of five and eight, I missed more school than I attended, although I was a very keen student. I passed the hours at home creating projects and reading one book after another, as well as completing all the school assignments I was missing. One year my teacher told my parents the top student in her class was the one who was very rarely there! I loved playing school with my dolls and teddies lined up in a row, listening attentively to every word I said. I never had to reprimand one of my students!

I remember being ill consistently for some months and being confined to bed. Mom and Dad moved my bed into the lounge to try to keep me connected to the hustle and bustle of everyday life and in the hopes of keeping up my spirits. However, over time, my health, and particularly my spirits, deteriorated greatly. When I look back, I think I must actually have been quite depressed, even though I was just seven years old. Throughout this experience, however, my dad was a constant source of love and support. He came home from his job and immediately sat at my bedside throughout the night. At my request, he would tell me one story after another to calm my breathing. "Tell me about the war, Daddy," I used to say, and he would start to regale the child-friendly versions of his experiences until I fell asleep. (Years later, when my first son, James, was born, his favorite thing to do when he was feeling ill was to lie down with "Da," his nickname for my dad, and have him tell stories about the war. Those stories never got old, and Dad never got tired of telling them.)

Every day at dawn, we listened for the little bird that appeared outside our window to sing. "There he is, Tooby. He's here to sing for you again," my dad would say. As I fell asleep, exhausted, Dad washed, dressed, and left the house, ready to begin a full day of work. Throughout all those years he never missed a day of work, and he never missed a full night of caring for me—though sometimes he did fall asleep in the middle of a sentence.

Things came to a head when, after a particularly bad asthma attack, my parents rushed me to the hospital. There I met Dr. Bound who, after many rather expensive tests that were a struggle for my parents to afford, diagnosed the triggers for my asthma. Among them were dust, fur, and feathers (we had a cat and a budgie at the time). He suggested we adopt out the animals and that I take up "singing or something," as the breathing techniques would be helpful to me. I do believe that encounter saved my life and moved me forward on the path I was destined to take. I was nine years old.

Isn't it true that our lives are a little like a jigsaw puzzle? Every experience, every relationship throughout our lives contributes another piece. My start in life had been a good, solid one. I had a family who loved me and a mom and dad who were very present in my life. I was well provided for. If I was to identify an area in which my background affected me negatively, it would be in confidence and self-esteem. I was born into a Northern England working-class mind-set of not getting "too big for your boots." Success was okay and even desired as long as you never forgot where you came from and didn't try to get "above your station." This idea was presented subversively, implied as opposed to stated openly, and never with an intent to hurt but rather, to control and protect one's environment.

My Dad was Adopted

My dad was adopted as a child. He found out when he asked for his birth certificate so he could enlist in the forces during WWII. He was eighteen years of age. Until then he had no idea his parents were anything other than his biological parents. He was, understandably, shocked, and it had a profound impact on his life. In those days, adoption was viewed in a completely different way. During the Victorian era in England, destitute orphans were looked down on, treated poorly, and often placed in workhouses, where there was barely enough food and clothing, and certainly no love and affection. Thank goodness times had changed in that regard. Dad was born in 1924, some twenty-five years after the Victorian era had ended. But there was enough remaining social stigma attached to adoption in some areas of the country to cause those with a prejudicial bent to raise their eyebrows over his "unknown" beginnings. Born to an unwed mother in Yorkshire who, from subsequent research of birth and adoption records, would appear came from a wealthy family, my dad was placed in an orphanage from birth and put up for adoption. Nine months later, he was placed in the home he subsequently grew up in. He was wanted, there is no doubt about that, and his adoptive parents were loving. But it was the attitude of others in that generation he would have to overcome. He became an overachiever and developed a need to want to keep the things that belonged to him—his family, for example—close to him.

A good sense of humor and a lovely smile, which made his eyes twinkle, is the memory I have of my dad in my childhood years. He was less inclined to share that side of his personality with those outside his immediate family. He was almost intimidated when he was out of the comfort of his own surroundings, so he was content to be with Mom and the three of us and make his family his life. It was safe, and it was comfortable. He was, quite rightly, proud of his accomplishments and the family he created. He was a hard worker and a "salt of the earth" man with a desire to build a better future for his brood. And he disliked arrogance or snobbery.

My First Singing Trophy

When I began singing in public, as a preteen and then into my teens and twenties, my father kept me grounded by being sparing with his compliments towards me. Although I can now see his justification for this lack of positive feedback, I acknowledge how much it hurt me, and I longed to please Daddy. I remember when I won my first singing trophy at the age of eleven. My dad was picking me up afterward. He worked long hours and was not able to be with me at the competition, so my grandma came with me. He was due to pick me up at 5:30 p.m. Because the newspaper wanted to take a picture of me for its coverage on the musical festival, I was delayed about half an hour. This was in the days of no cell phones, so I could not communicate the reason for the delay ahead of time. When I finally arrived at the pick-up spot, Dad was furious. I remember getting in the car and saying, "Dad, I won! I won the trophy!" All I got in response was, "You're late!" And he never said another word all the way home. I longed to hear him say, "I'm so proud of you. You're wonderful. I love you." These are all things I have since said to my own children when they have accomplished something they have worked hard for.

Suffice it to say I know he meant no malice. I knew he loved me, but I longed to hear him actually say it. These days, people tell me all the time how he's told them how proud he is of me and talks at length about my accomplishments. I'd love to hear it for myself! In spite of having a mom and dad who generously gave of their time and money to ensure I had everything I needed, the lack of overt praise and vocal validation did have, and continues to have, a profound effect on my life. My need for validation from those around me has shaped many choices I have made and many fears I have developed throughout my life. I do not love my mom and dad any less for it. They did their best for me, and I adore them and am so grateful for all the sacrifices they made for me. But more than anything, I am beyond grateful that they first introduced me to a loving Savior, who I ultimately, many years later, claimed as my own. He daily works within my life and through the lives of others he has placed around me—not least my husband—to free me from the constraints I place on myself as a result of these experiences. God affirms and reaffirms that in His eyes, I am wonderful, the daughter of a King. I can deal with that!

"Sisters, Sisters, There Were Never Such Devoted Sisters" (White Christmas)

Joy, my sister, began taking singing lessons when she was sixteen. She quickly became proficient and began singing solos at church regularly. I thought she was amazing, and I wanted to be like her so much. My trip to the ER had come at a timely moment for, when Joy left home to get married at nineteen, I moved straight into her much-coveted time slot with her singing teacher, Audrey Brearley. I loved being taught by Miss Brearley. She lived in an old Victorian mansion in St Annes on Sea, and she knew exactly how to bring out the best in your voice. I was always a little fearful of her. Is that such a bad thing? So I practiced what I was told to practice and did my homework dutifully. And I improved.

As I look back on those years, I can see exactly how the Lord brought people into my life at just the right time. I really believe this has been a consistent thing throughout my life. Whether it was to bring physical healing (Dr. Bound) care, (my parents) or someone to nourish and encourage my musical ability (Miss Brearley), there truly was the right time for every one of these encounters.

Within the walls of my church, there was an opportunity to sing as a child and to be affirmed in the gift God gave me. Even school, although not a Christian environment (I do believe it's not always the Christians God uses to fulfill His plan!) gave me a training ground to grow and develop my singing ability. By the age of ten I was playing the piano reasonably well and spent hours accompanying myself singing. It was my favorite pastime. Mr. Williams, my fourth-grade teacher, encouraged me to sing and play as he harmonized tunes on his recorder over a rainy lunchtime or when the weather was too cold for me to go to play (it would trigger an asthma attack). Those times are fond memories, as are the Gilbert and Sullivan operettas presented by the top elementary class each year at Stanley Junior School, my elementary school. This huge undertaking with such relatively young children was directed by the imposing headmaster Percy Hall. It was in this environment I grew to love musicals and theater.

"The Gondoliers"

The year it was my turn to participate in the school musical it was *The Gondoliers,* and I played the part of Tessa. I sang,

> When a Merry Maiden Marries,
> Sorrow goes and pleasure tarries,
> Every smile becomes a song,
> All is right and nothing's wrong!

I couldn't wait to get into costume and step out onto the stage. Other children might suffer from stage fright. Not me! I counted down the minutes to show-time and built my whole day around the event. I suffered from "post-show lag" when *The Gondoliers* wrapped. The review of the show was printed in the newspaper the next evening. It read, "and the audience was lucky to spot a new star in the ascent. I predict that, if Barbara Sharp [my maiden name] so chooses, she will make a real name for herself in dramatic circles" (*The Evening Gazette*). I was completely hooked!

I continued to act and sing in musical theater productions, playing most of the female leads in the Gilbert and Sullivan library of operettas, a plethora of "Songs from the Shows" productions as well as Oliver in *Oliver Twist,* Charlie in *Charlie Girl,* and my personal favorite of all time, Eliza in *My Fair Lady.*

"Some Day My Prince Will Come" (Snow White)

I don't know whether you believe in a soul mate - that certain someone God has for you. In my case, I do, and his name is Steve Allen. He has been a part of my life since I was five years old. Actually before then, but I don't recollect our first meeting. Our families were friends and attended the same church, and our moms were pregnant with us at the same time. The story goes that Steve's parents ran into mine in the park just after he was born, and my mom was nearing her due date to give birth to me. After the usual cooing that goes along with seeing a newborn, the two couples allegedly joked about how funny it would be if my parents had a girl and the two children ended up getting married some day. Too cute! As very young children, we played together at each other's houses when our parents met up for an evening. Most New Year's Eves were spent together, celebrating with our families. Through our teenage love/hate years to getting engaged at twenty-one years of age (only to break it off shortly afterward), Steve and I were a pair.

Steve studied trombone at Chethams Music School but was also a fine pianist. As kids, we played pianoforte duets together, sang together, and sat next to each other in the trombone section of our church band. We were a real team—when we weren't arguing.

In 1979, when we were both nineteen, we traveled to California to visit some friends from church, who had recently immigrated to the States and living in Sacramento. In those days, very few people from the UK ventured as far as the west coast of America, so it was truly an adventure. It was also love at first sight! We visited the Golden Gate Bridge, Sausalito, Alcatraz, and even drove to Southern California to visit Disneyland and Magic Mountain. It was a wonderful vacation. I felt so drawn to California that I could not settle once I returned. I would dream about it and wake up disappointed to find I was no longer there! I vowed that one day I would live in California. I little realized the implication of that vow or even recognized it for what, with hindsight, I believe it was—the foundation of a calling the Lord was placing on my heart. But first, He had a lot of work to do in my life.

Mr. Steve Allen

Steve Allen has always been an adventurer and a visionary. He has a magnetic personality that draws people to him. It doesn't take much for a small, eager group of listeners to gather around when he's recounting an adventure or an experience in an impromptu setting. That's only part of the attraction! He's a kind, caring, compassionate person with a twinkle in his eye and a fabulous sense of humor.

Never one to shirk the opportunity for adventure, Steve headed off to work at a summer camp the following year. It was situated in New York, and the arrangement was that I would work through the summer and earn enough money to travel to New York and join him for a vacation once his employment had finished. I remember counting down the days, hardly able to stand the waiting. As soon as I got off the plane, I noticed almost immediately the difference in this person I knew so well. Remember, Steve and I had virtually grown up together, and as the proverbial childhood sweethearts, we knew each other pretty well. Something was different. It wasn't long before I found what it was. Steve was saved. Now I was no stranger to the Lord. I had grown up in a family of churchgoers, but this was different. He was different. I wasn't so sure I liked it. He spoke at length about his experience and how it had given him a purpose and direction for his life. That week of vacation was not what I had expected, and although I wasn't exactly against this transformation, I couldn't understand why it had to permeate everything. Why couldn't it just be contained to certain areas of his life and kept under control?

It was a rocky week to say the least, but not a deal breaker for me. There was still so much to love about him, so I guessed I could put up with this! Steve returned to our hometown to talk to his peer group at church about his time in New York and finding salvation. It ignited a flame that literally roared through the young people of our church over the next months and years. And it spoke loudly and clearly to me. The youth of our church began holding regular, in-depth Bible studies and forums to discuss the things that affected us as young people and the Bible's teaching regarding these issues. Testimonies were regularly and freely shared with anyone who would listen, and every so often, all-night prayer meetings were held. One Sunday evening, at a youth fellowship service led by our young people at a small neighborhood church, I dedicated my life to Christ. I was twenty years old, and I believe this was the turning point in my life.

"I Did It My Way" (Frank Sinatra)

As I look back, I can see so many times when I didn't understand why something happened, or if it really should have happened at all. I guess that age brings wisdom, and retrospect is a wonderful thing. But now I see the purpose of opportunities and disappointments that came my way in my teens and twenties, even though at the time, it seemed a hopeless mess. God is at work in and through every experience. I was—and am—His child, bought at a great price, and He had a plan for me. All those wrong decisions and misdirections would be harnessed by him and used for the good. He was not about to let me get away!

Of course, these statements are written with the benefit of seeing how God worked it out so far. But even now, I have a tendency to try to fix things myself, in my own strength. I have to remind myself we are promised sufficient strength and grace one day at a time. When I read the story of Moses and the people of Israel in the wilderness, journeying toward the Promised Land, I completely understand their frustration in worrying about their food for the next week instead of just waiting to receive the daily manna promised to them. Our society encourages us to rely on ourselves as the creator of each experience, with little regard for the plan or purpose God has in mind for us. "That's a great idea, God, but have you thought about this? I think I'd like that much better!" That's our humanness, I suppose, and it's a struggle to "let go and let God," even though He created us and knows us much better than we think we know ourselves. All this is to say finding salvation does not mean a smooth ride into eternity. My grandma's favorite song at church has some poetic verbiage, which I quite delight in and have claimed many times throughout the years.

> I do not ask Thee, Lord
> That all my life may be
> An easy smooth and pleasant path, It would not be good for me.
> But, Oh I ask today that grace and strength be given
> To keep me fighting all the way that leads to God and Heaven.

I met Chris at the Operatic Society. He was not a Christian, but he was a nice person and we got along well. I obviously hadn't read the passage of Scripture about being unequally yoked. Steve and I had broken our engagement, so I was looking to date again, primarily to teach him a lesson and let him see what he was missing! Chris and I shared similar interests, and we were like best friends. So we got engaged. Just like that. In fact, being someone who could dig their heels in to prove a point, I even brought the wedding forward in answer to my parents' and siblings' voiced concerns. Steve was going back to California (there it is again!) to work another summer.

My Wedding to Chris

It was June 1984, one month before my wedding to Chris, when I bumped into Steve in town. All the uncertainties about the decision I was making ran through my head as we talked and laughed about "old times." I knew something wasn't quite right, and so did he. Cue: Perhaps, call off the wedding? Not at all! It was too late, *wasn't it?* If this happened to me now, I wouldn't hesitate, but I was twenty-three and fearful of "upsetting the applecart," as the saying goes. So I dismissed it and moved forward, carrying the niggling doubts with me. Fast forward to Sunday evening, the final time Steve would be around before flying off to Los Angeles. He spotted me across the room looking a little downcast and mouthed, "Are you okay?"

I shook my head. According to Steve, he planned to catch up with me later and let me know how he felt. He wanted to ask me to wait and not go ahead with the wedding. However, I left early, so he sought out my mom. He asked her to convey his feelings— that he loved me, wanted to marry me, and would return in a few months. I never got the message. I married Chris on July 21, 1984, while Steve, six thousand miles away, sat in silence on a grassy bank and threw stones in a pond, wondering why I didn't respond to his message.

"Don't Put Your Daughter on the Stage, Mrs. Worthington!" (Noel Coward)

My marriage to Chris lasted nine months, and only that long because it took so long for the divorce to be finalized. It was over before it began, and I knew the minute I said, "I do," I had made a huge mistake. I am remorseful to this day that I didn't heed the warnings of my family or seek divine guidance on any level. What was I thinking?

So began a two-year tailspin that, even now, is very foggy. It's as if I've been protected from the pain of it all, and for that I am grateful. I have fully accepted and "owned it." I see the sin clearly for what it was and deeply regret the hurt I must have inflicted on so many people caught in the crossfire, not least Chris.

Over the next couple years, I continued with singing, though not at church. I stopped attending, feeling very rebellious and disillusioned. I was working during the day as a music teacher and singing professionally at night in theaters and clubs. I learned many valuable skills regarding communicating with audiences during that time that would come to bear fruit much later. That's probably the only positive thing I gleaned from this time in my life. It was a dark time but not without those fleeting moments of respite, when someone would speak a word of truth via letter, phone call, or word of mouth. I am so grateful for those people from my church who were moved to stay in touch and held out a lifeline to me, even when I did not respond. They were true angels and integral to my emotional recovery as I struggled to come to terms with where my life was heading.

I was unsettled in my world, though I loved teaching children. Seeing my work on productions of shows such as *Oliver, Aladdin,* and *Sleeping Beauty* come to life with these precious kids playing their roles with confidence and surety was cathartic. I loved working with them, honing their music and drama skills, and ultimately moved to tears when I saw them take their bows to rapturous applause. This was how I had started, and I loved being able to cultivate this in a future generation. It got me through those tough days.

Open Casting Call

I had always wanted to work in television. There is just something about it that inspires me. The minute I walk into a studio, I get such a buzz of excitement that I can't wait to get in front of the camera. Until now, I never believed I had the ability to land a gig on TV, but things had changed. I had changed. I responded to an open casting call in a British entertainment newspaper called *The Stage*, the go-to periodical for the industry. So one Wednesday morning, I wended my way to Manchester, much to the chagrin of my mom and dad, who did not want me to be involved in this line of work at all. I had written a song called "You" and thought it might be a bit different to sing and play the piano, performing my own composition so as to stand out a little from all the other singers there to audition. This was the era of *Opportunity Knocks,* a very popular though somewhat staid talent show in the UK. *New Faces* was the updated, more modern, and more elaborately produced offspring and a precursor of today's *Britain's Got Talent* and ultimately *America's Got Talent*. I have read that Simon Cowell, just a young guy at the time, was inspired to create his talent shows by watching *New Faces* back in the '80s!

At the audition venue, I touched up my hair and makeup in the bathroom before I was called in for audition. I actually prayed silently the opportunity would be mine if, "it was meant for me." I hadn't done that for a while, God probably answered, "and about time, too!" After the audition in front of the producer, director, and musical director, I drove home satisfied that at least I had tried, and I thought no more about it.

I lived in my brother's house at the time, as Kevin was also recently divorced. This arrangement worked well for both of us because we were really ships that passed in the night. I don't think there were more than a couple of times (one being New Year's Eve, when we both cried at the stroke of midnight!) that we were home at the same time. It was definitely a shelter in the midst of my storm and his. In this age of cell phones, voice mails, e-mails, texts, and Twitter, it's difficult to remember what it was like to have just one phone in the house and no voice message recorder. But that's how it was. So when the phone rang on my way out the door one morning, it came as a surprise to hear the voice of the producer's assistant from *New Faces* on the other end of the line. "We've been trying to reach you for weeks," she said, "and this was our last attempt. We would like you to appear on the show in week six of the series." I was floored. I spluttered something in the way of thanks and headed out of the door dumbfounded but bursting to tell someone, anyone, about this amazing turn of events.

The next few weeks were filled with meetings with the costume department; the musical director for the show, Keith Strachan, who would be writing the twenty-six-piece orchestral accompaniment to my song; and the wonderful, charming orchestral conductor, Harry Rabinowitz. It was a whirlwind, and I loved it!

Birmingham Hippodrome was the venue for the show, and I spent a couple of days holed up in a hotel, attending rehearsals and dinners in anticipation of the show taping. I was beyond happy to be a part of this adventure. On the day of the taping, the audience filled the seats. Each seat was equipped with a button to vote for your favorite artist. Each vote illuminated a bulb on the big scoreboard called "spaghetti junction," after the famous roadways crisscrossing the Birmingham area. The person with the longest line of lights would win through to the next round and secure a place in the final. In rehearsal, we all took our turns as the potential winner, stepping out on to the catwalk and receiving the applause of the audience, just in case. I loved my dress, taffeta and a beautiful jade green—so 1987! This, together with a white baby grand piano that slowly moved downstage as I played and sang, were all pretty very cool.

My *Performance* — *I won!*

The performance went without a hitch, and it was time for the votes to be cast. I scanned the audience, trying to take it all in. It would soon all be over, and this would be nothing more than a memory. They mentioned my name "Barbara Allan" (this was my stage name at the time), and I watched the lights fly around Spaghetti Junction, slowing as they came level with another act and then continuing beyond. I held my breath. I'd won! I stepped forward to receive the applause with a huge smile on my face. I could not believe it. There were two parts to the voting, part one came from the studio audience and part two from viewers at home. In those days, they had to mail in their votes. Imagine that; what a lot of effort. But nonetheless, people did it—in the thousands! You had to win both voting groups to advance to the final, and I wouldn't know until the middle of the week. The call came on the Wednesday. I made it. Special thanks at this time should go to all the children and their families at the school where I was working who voted for me! They were stellar supporters. The previous week's winner was officially announced live at the start of the next round of the show, and I was not at liberty to disclose it until then.

So where was God in all this, you might ask. Oh, He was working all right. *New Faces* provided a much-needed distraction from the funk I had been in for so long, and gestures of encouragement and congratulations rekindled some lost relationships I was the poorer for not having in my life. Slowly but surely, the pieces of the jigsaw puzzle were being put in place for what lay ahead.

"I'm Getting Married in the Morning" (My Fair Lady)

It must have been a couple of months later, after the show and before the final, when I ran into Steve again. I had not seen him for five years. We were standing near a local pub, it was lunchtime, and we were freezing (it was winter), so we ducked inside for a bite to eat and a chat. Enter a second major turning point in my life, strangely enough, emanating from the same person as the first.

After enjoying our lunch, we grabbed a coffee and began to chat. We caught up on the events of the past five years and had a wonderful time reconnecting. Steve was working as a probation officer and attending a different church, a very charismatic one much different from our childhood church. At one point in the conversation, he pushed an ashtray in front of me. It was filled with cigarette butts and smelled dreadful. On the other side of the table he placed a key fob (he had just got a new car, and the keys were new and shiny). He said, "The problem is, Barb, you keep making the wrong choices. You keep choosing the ugly things in life [gesturing to the ashtray] instead of the glorious things God has for you [the shiny keys]." Of course, he didn't mean God had a new car waiting for me if I'd just repent, but you catch my drift! It was as if a light-bulb went on for the first time in years. No great profound statement, but all the times others had spoken truth into my life had led to this moment. It was the final link in the chain. I was ready to change.

Mr. and Mrs. Steve Allen

I began attending Steve's church with him and eventually made my way back "home." Steve was in the front row for my appearance on the *New Faces* live finale as I sang my new composition, "Taking a Chance Again," a song I had written especially for him. It did not take long for us to decide we wanted to be together, and on Valentine's Day, wearing that much-loved jade green dress, I said yes to his proposal. We were married on August 20, 1988, in the middle of a twenty-six-week summer season of performances at the Palladium Theater. The children's choir, who had so faithfully voted for me, sang "Father, Hear Our Prayer." He certainly had!

Twelve months saw a lot of change in our lives. Coming alongside me as the doctor for my professional singing career, Steve was, and is, a wonderfully supportive and loving husband—a true gift from God. We welcomed James, our firstborn son in 1989 and then Jordan in 1991. Life was settled again … or so we thought!

Barbara and Steve Allen on their wedding day

"This Land is Your Land, This Land Is My Land" (Woody Guthrie)

Steve and I felt called to return to our childhood church and took up leadership roles in that community for several years. But both of us sensed the Lord's calling on our lives. Established in our careers and living comfortably, there was an unsettling longing for something, though we were not sure what. All we knew was that we felt we should be serving elsewhere.

Time passed, and the boys were growing up. James was four and Jordan two when we decided to explore the possibilities of the place that had meant so much to us all those years ago: California. We believed that if this was indeed the place we should be, there would be a clear directive. I wrote to a contact in Northern California, expressing our thoughts, and got no response. A further six months passed. One evening when the boys were asleep, Steve and I sat down and talked about our future. We discussed the idea of "putting a fleece out" to help us clarify what the Lord wanted us to do, so that's exactly what we did. I suggested we pray some kind of correspondence from the States arriving on our doormat on Friday morning (mail is pushed through the door in the UK) to let us know we should pursue this avenue. I know that sounds a little off, but that's exactly what we did. Granted, this was already Monday, and no one would have the chance to write that letter, mail it, and get it to us by Friday, even if the Lord tapped the person on the shoulder at that very moment to start the ball rolling.

Tuesday came and went and then Wednesday and Thursday. Steve checked the doormat diligently—and somewhat skeptically, I might add...still no mail. Friday morning dawned, and following his pattern for the previous few days, Steve nonchalantly checked the mat, presuming the results would be the same. He returned holding a letter from Northern California, apologizing for the delay in responding but offering to look into our request. You might say that was a done deal. However, following that amazing revelation, everything went silent again for another twelve months! We were obviously being taught patience.

Have you ever heard the saying, "The Lord helps those who help themselves"? Twelve months to the day the letter was received, Steve picked up the phone and spoke to a contact in Southern California. He recounted the whole story one more time. Within two weeks, we were flying to Pasadena, California, to sing at a special charity event following the Northridge earthquake disaster. During that weekend (yes, we traveled six thousand miles for a weekend and were both back at work on Monday morning), we were offered employment as co-creative ministries directors. We were stunned. That quickly? Why not? When God moves, He is methodical and takes care of everything in His time. We rented out our home a week before we left and sold our car the night before. We just had to remember the manna in the desert.

December 29, 1994, saw us bidding a very tearful good-bye to both sides of the family and boarding a flight for Los Angeles for the start of a new chapter of our lives.

"Just Where He Needs Me, My Lord Had Placed Me" (Miriam M. Richards)

The transition was not easy. Finding a school for James and a preschool for Jordan in a strange country would have been an insurmountable problem had it not been for the kind, generous spirit of Catherine, a lady from our new church. She took two weeks out of her life to help me create a home for mine. I am still friends with her these nineteen years later, and I will never forget her compassion as she walked me through those difficult first few weeks of acclimation.

With the boys happily ensconced in great schools, God's provision continued. Our six-month rent-free apartment freed up funds for the tuition costs needed for the boys. And when that time ran out, we were working as camp director and Christian education director at a Christian summer camp in Calabasas, which provided free housing and food for the next three months. What's more, the boys had a blast participating in all the camp activities surrounded by the beauty and majesty of the rugged terrain. We did, however, hold our breath a few times as three-year-old Jordan rode his little tricycle, which had no brakes on it, to the top of the hill in camp and launched himself downhill, legs akimbo, whooping with delight! It was a wonderful summer.

Our beloved James and Jordan

Moving Again

Fall 1995 saw us moving again. This time to a house with affordable rent and was associated with our jobs and situated right across the street from a good public school. Things finally seemed to be settling down as we adjusted to our new life in the States. Then our jobs folded.

"Hold Me Jesus, 'cause I'm Shaking Like a Leaf, You Have Been King of My Glory, Won't You Be My Prince of Peace?" (Richard Mullins)

It's devastating to lose a job, but it's a whole other shade of devastating when both of you lose your jobs and you're trying to function in a strange country with two young children. To add insult to injury, the house we had moved into just nine months before as part of the employment agreement was also going to be unavailable to us in the same budget-cut decision. Now I fully understand the need to cut budgets when that, indeed, is what is happening. But there was a little more to it than that. It revolved around a change in leadership and a long-standing disagreement between the outgoing leadership and the incoming. It wasn't about us, or even our ability to fulfill the employment we had been given; we were clearly told we had done a wonderful job. It was all a personal disagreement and we were caught in the crossfire between the two individuals.

We were told we had one month to find other employment and move out of the house. Rendered a little paralyzed by the seemingly heartless nature of the decision, we started to pray. My mother-in-law and father-in-law were visiting us at the time and had one week of vacation left. The timing could not have been better, as my mother-in-law is a staunch prayer warrior. Every morning before we left for work that week, we held hands in a circle and prayed the Lord would help us make some sense of this travesty and show us a way forward.

Things moved swiftly. God brought two wonderfully supportive men from our church to our sides, both eloquent and well versed in the workings of the church, and the legal restrictions regarding employment provisions promised to us and to the US Immigration Service on application for our visas. Steve and I did not feel defeated. We felt supernaturally empowered, certain that God had this in hand. He sure did! First, we won a grievance against the perpetrator of this turn of events. Steve worked closely with the two guys who volunteered their support, and together, they put forward such a profound and effective argument there was no option but for the party concerned to concede.

Steve received a placement similar to the arena in which he had worked before we immigrated, with a substantial pay raise. Meanwhile, I was offered work at a Christian school as head of music. I had actually been approached about that job a week before this traumatic turn of events even began. Whoever heard of a teaching job being available on November 1? Especially as the previous teacher had just been hired to start in September and then suddenly quit in October! Not only that, it was at the school I had initially wanted to get James into, but they had no openings. Miraculously (yes, it was a miracle), they had just one spot available in first grade, and that was the grade James was in.

As for somewhere to live, another gentleman at church, on hearing of our situation, informed us his neighbors were looking for a new tenant for their beautiful, single-story home in San Gabriel, which was a short commute to the school and preschool for the boys. I realized God doesn't just provide, He lavishes His provision on us more than we could ever imagine. And so we happily began the next chapter of our lives.

"I'm Trading My Sorrows, I'm Trading My Pain" (Darrell Evans)

By 2000, we had settled in a lovely town called Glendora, nestled at the foothill of the San Gabriel Valley mountain range. A more picturesque town you could not wish to see, and we loved it. However, all was not well at the church, and it was very unsettling to Steve and me. We began to pray about where the Lord needed us to be if it wasn't in California. We were truly willing to leave all we had become accustomed to so we could be in His will. We continued this way for some months, and I, for one, was becoming very unsettled and somewhat disillusioned with the way things were.

Moving to Australia?

It was a Thursday evening, and the phone rang at home. At the other end was a pastor from Sydney, who, out of the blue, offered us employment in Australia. I was offered the music director position at the church in Sydney (a pioneering move for that particular church denomination), and Steve had the opportunity to head up the Social Services Department over there. We flew to Sydney the following week to be officially interviewed and to have a look around for a house and schools. It was a whirlwind of a week. The people in leadership at the church were delightful and so enthusiastic about the new direction they were taking. We were bowled over with their hospitality and grateful for this answer to prayer.

After the formalities in Sydney were completed, all that was left was for us to come back to the States, sell the house, and move lock, stock, and barrel. We shared the news with the boys, who were eight and ten at the time. Their understanding was somewhat limited, but they were ready for the adventure. We decided we would sell the house, I would give notice at my place of employment a semester in advance (I still worked at the Christian school), and we would move to Sydney at the end of August. The house went on the market in a property climate that was hot, hot, hot! It was the millennium boom, when available houses in Glendora were few and far between, and sold in a matter of days. We lived in a charming 2,600-square-foot home with a white wooden fence on a leafy lane. "Who wouldn't want to buy this?" the realtor told us. She even put a sign on the for sale board, stating, "I'm gorgeous inside!"

We expected to receive an offer in probably no more than a week or so, and we would be on our way. Nothing … absolutely nothing. The house was priced correctly and in move-in condition. Everything was in place, except the buyer. And so it stayed for three months. The realtor could not understand it, but we could. We had been feeling uncertain about this move since we got back from Australia. It wasn't the same as when we moved from the UK. This move was different and just didn't feel right. The putting out a fleece idea had worked beautifully last time, so we thought we'd do it again. If we didn't sell the house by the end of August, we would not move. July and August came and went—nothing. On August 31, we picked up the phone to the pastor in Sydney and said we were not coming. He was so kind and understanding. He offered to extend the period of waiting to the end of the year, but we just knew. We actually had no idea why we were meant to stay. Life at church was not good, and now I had no job. Fortunately, Steve had not handed in his resignation. We weren't sure how this would work out, but God knew.

The millennial year turned out to be a glorious one for our family. The boys attended the local public schools. Without the staff tuition break I had received as a teacher, we could not afford to send them to the Christian school. They developed friendships with other students that year that they enjoy to this day; a couple of them, our youngest son, Jordan, had the privilege of leading to the Lord during high school. They are still a welcome addition to our family when they come over to hang out. I was not working full time, so I could drop the boys at school and pick them up. With only one income, there was no rational explanation for how we afforded to pay our bills and keep the same standard of living except by the power of God's provision. Our needs were met from day to day, and we were never without. We had been willing to sacrifice to be in the center of the Lord's will, and that was all He needed to know. He didn't really want us to move, just be willing to go.

From this period on, our lives blossomed into some incredible blessings that, as I reflect on them, bring tears to my eyes. Through the turmoil at church came peace and a desire to begin a music ministry involving the teens and twenties that would involve music they could embrace and use to communicate to others. We are both still leaders of the youth chorus. James uses his considerable musical talents to arrange music for us and to provide accompaniment on the keyboard or drums. Jordan, who found his gift of singing just a few years ago, is one of the group's soloists. We have been blessed through the difficulties and never cease to be amazed at how the Lord can lead us from the valleys of life to a mountaintop from which we can see His working in our lives so clearly.

"Strength for Today and Bright Hope for Tomorrow, Blessings All Mine with Ten Thousand Beside" ("Great Is Thy Faithfulness," by Thomas Chisholm, inspired by Lamentations 3:22-23)

This year, 2013, will be our nineteenth year of living in California. For the past fifteen years, I have worked as a performing arts consultant and vocal coach, and this has brought me great joy.

The childhood memories of my first "show" have inspired me to re-create the experience for children, young people, and adults who love musical theater. I have had the privilege of directing and producing some twenty-five shows. From casting call to final curtain, they have been a labor of love and pure joy. In creating Camera-Ready Choirs, my work has brought me into contact with many wonderfully talented singers and the opportunity to work in television once again on such shows as *America's Got Talent, American Music Awards, Dancing with the Stars,* and *American Idol.* I have worked with such artists as Andrea Bocelli, David Foster, Susan Boyle, Michael Bolton, Jackie Evancho, and Katy Perry.

In addition, I have had the privilege of many wonderful opportunities to sing for the Lord in many different parts of the world. My early dreams of singing professionally have morphed with my ministry, and I continue to be amazed at the doors that are opened—not least this opportunity to share my testimony in print.

Steve and I have been privileged to travel throughout the US, UK, South America, Canada, Australia, and New Zealand, using our music as a means of communicating the gospel to others. Sometimes we do grow a little weary as we try to balance our everyday lives and employment with the demands of ministry and travel, like the time in Woollongong, Australia, when Steve was so overcome with jetlag that he fell asleep at the keyboard between my songs! In Chile we taught at a music school where the students had traveled on a non-air-conditioned bus for five days from Ecuador, Bolivia, and Peru just to be a part of it. And in the Marshall Islands, we met with Christian young people who sang from their very souls. The sound of their voices is something I will never forget.

These experiences have been an inspiration to us. Steve and I have been married for twenty-five years, and we look forward to many more together! Our boys are now young men. James, twenty-four, is a professional musician and has met and married the woman God planned for him, Priscilla. Music brought them together, and they minister in the youth chorus together. She is everything I could have ever wanted in a loving, nurturing daughter-in-law with a heart who loves the Lord. They are blessed to have found each other and will, in turn, be a blessing to many others in the years ahead. Jordan, twenty-two, is an aspiring, talented filmmaker, who has dedicated his gifts to the Lord and has a desire to walk with Him. He recognizes the doors the Lord has opened for Him and seeks God's will for His life. His singing can be heard at all times of the day (and night) throughout our home. In recent years, he and I have enjoyed recording and performing together. Our family is a joy and a delight to Steve and me.

We are so grateful to have both sets of our parents alive. The distance between us is a sacrifice we still have to deal with, especially as advanced age has brought health concerns. Steve's father, Bryan, was diagnosed with Parkinson's disease, but ever the upbeat, strong believer he is, he keeps us—and himself—laughing with his witticisms and self-deprecating humor. My mother-in-law is a strong woman of God, who bears her burdens with grace and dignity. They are both wonderful people, whom I admire and love greatly. My mom was diagnosed with Alzheimer's ten years ago and now has no recollection of most of our shared memories. On a visit to her, I found the one constant that can reach her is music. Together we sang through every childhood Sunday school chorus we had ever learned. She remembered every word and even sang the harmony lines! I was amazed and greatly comforted by that spark of recollection. As for Dad, he looks twenty-five years younger than his eighty-nine years after his heart valve replacement in 2012. He can still spin a good war tale but struggles with loneliness and greatly misses my mom's companionship and conversation. He visits her every day. They have been married for sixty-six years.

God's provision is central to my life. He has proved His love for me time and time again, and I know in my heart His strength is so much better than my strength and His grace so much more far reaching than I deserve or can comprehend. My challenges have not been the devastating, life-threatening ones other people have had to face. And for that, I am so grateful. However, I have still had challenges that have affected my life's path, and for that,

I am even more grateful. God's provision for me is often taken for granted when all is going well. I am guilty of overlooking God's grace when all is going according to plan—my plan. When I have not been able to see through the darkness, those are the times I have felt the closest to my Lord. This world drowns out so much of His voice. I hope, in the time it has taken for you to read this narrative, you will have felt His peace surround you in the midst of your storm, whatever that may be. I am so grateful for the tremendous blessings in my life, not least a husband who loves me unconditionally and always has my back. I thank God for bringing people into my life who have spoken truth and ministered to me when I was lost. I am a living, breathing example of God's love for His children and His abundant provision for them.

The Lord has placed a song in my heart, and I am blessed to sing it. My prayer for the future is that I may be faithful and diligent in my ministry, used by the Lord as a channel to bring comfort, encouragement, and, God willing, open a door to the Father's love for those who do not know Him.

I was born to sing.

The entire Allen family 2013

My Testimony

In my moments of fear, through every pain every tear
There's a God whose been faithful to me
When my strength was all gone,
And when my heart it had no song
Still in love, He was faithful to me
Every word He promised, is true
What I thought was impossible
I see my God do
He's been faithful, faithful to me
Looking back His love and mercy I see
In my heart I would question, even fail to believe
But He's been faithful, faithful to me.

Carol Cymbala

You can contact Barbara Allen on Facebook or at
Barballen2012@gmail.com.

PROVERBS 31 *"Virtuous Wife"* vs. 10 - 31

[10] Who can find a virtuous wife, for her worth is far above rubies.

[11] The heart of her husband safely trusts her, so he will have no lack of gain.

[12] She does him good and not evil all the days of her life.

[13] She seeks wool and flax, and willingly works with her hands.

[14] She is like the merchant ships, she brings her food from afar.

[15] She also rises while it is yet night, and provides food for her household, and a portion for her maidservants.

[16] She considers a field and buys it; from her profits she plants a vineyard.

[17] She girds herself with strength, and strengthens her arms.

[18] She perceives that her merchandise is good, and her lamp does not go out by night.

[19] She stretches out her hands to the distaff, and her hands hold the spindle.

[20] She extends her hand to the poor, yes, she reaches out her hands to the needy.

[21] She is not afraid of snow for her household, for her household is clothed in scarlet.

[22] She makes tapestry for herself, her clothing is fine linen and purple.

[23] Her husband is known in the gates, when he sits among the elders of the land.

[24] She makes linen garments and sells them, and supplies sashes for the merchants.

[25] Strength and honor are her clothing, she shall rejoice in time to come.

[26] She opens her mouth with wisdom, and on her tongue is the law of kindness.

[27] She watches over the ways of her household, and does not eat the bread of idleness.

[28] Her children rise up and call her blessed; her husband also, and he praises her:

[29] "Many daughters have done well, but you excel them all."

[30] Charm is deceitful and beauty is passing, but a woman who fears the Lord, she shall be praised.

[31] Give her of the fruit of her hands, and let her own works praise her in the gates.

Proverbs 31: The "Virtuous Wife"

The Beloved Bride of Christ

– BY SHAUNA MAYER

Photo and permission by Janet Barnett,
Barnett Lifestyles Photography, 2013.

Warrior Princess: Daughter of the King of Kings

Why do we, as women, love to hate the Proverbs 31 Woman? In my opinion, it's because she's written as a modern-day "Martha" type, incessantly driven and an extreme overachiever. Living in her shadow makes the rest of us look bad, right? Why? Because she is obviously blessed, highly favored, and successful at *all* she puts her hands to. I'd like to be accused of that!

What kind of *'confession'* does she have to make as a Christian wife? You're probably thinking, *this is an OT Scripture, how could this possibly have anything to do with Jesus and being a Christian wife?* If she could speak for herself, she'd say, "As the Proverbs 31 Woman and a virtuous wife, I am different than you think I am and more than you know." Let me explain.

Introduced to the Proverbs 31 Woman

Once a year, the Women's Ministry at my church would have a Sunday evening where our pastor's wife, Anna Hayford, and the women's team ministered to the women and then anointed and prayed for everyone. How we, as women, looked forward to that special evening. One year, I was sitting at the very back of the large sanctuary. Anna finally approached me, anointed my head, and said emphatically, "Lord, give this woman a ministry!" We barely knew each other, so I can only assume she said that because she'd seen me so often serving at the church. I volunteered as often as I was able and in many different capacities over the years.

"A ministry," she'd said. I was flattered by her prayer for me, but the simple truth was I didn't want to minister or be in ministry. I had no desire to lead; I just wanted to serve. The idea of taking on a leadership role of any kind wasn't on my radar screen at all.

In January of the following year, 1996, Chip and I had the great privilege of sharing our testimonies of God's deliverance, healing, and salvation in our lives on a TBN telecast. The anointing of God was powerful during the taping and throughout the remainder of the day. I still felt the weight of His presence later that night, and I couldn't go to sleep. I felt the tug of the Lord to get out of bed and read the Bible. So I did. While reading the Word, I experienced what one might call a visitation from the Lord. As I sat on the couch in the living room, with my Bible open on my lap, I heard Him say, "Turn to Proverbs 31. This is your ministry; of women, by women and for women." For about two hours, I was keenly aware of the direction He was giving me and a vision of a plan and purpose for His ministry that I was to follow. It was a very memorable night. It changed my life forever. I wasn't familiar with the Proverbs 31 chapter at that time, but it sure wouldn't take long to find out what *everyone else* thought about this Proverbs 31 Woman, though.

First the Vision, then the Provision

About three years before, the Lord told me in my sleep, "First will come the vision, then the provision." I was completely baffled by those words. What could that have meant? Proverbs 4:7 says, **"Wisdom is the principal thing; therefore get wisdom, And in all your getting, get understanding."** I now had a vision based on what He'd said to me. But I had only the slightest understanding of what lay ahead for me. Women's ministry! I was surprised, but nonetheless, I was off and running the race set before me!

"Oh, I Hate that Woman!"

The next time I saw Anna Hayford at church, I literally ran to her, utterly amazed the Lord had actually honored her prayer and given me a ministry. I told her, "Anna, God gave me a ministry."

She stopped, listened, and then asked with loving curiosity, "What is it?" "It's the Proverbs 31 Woman," I said joyfully. Naively. She took a beat and smiled in her sweet way. "Oh, I hate that woman!" she said with a little twinkle in her eye.

What? I was shocked by her response. I stood there, speechless. It wasn't the first time I had received that reaction as I joyfully shared my good news about "my" ministry. *What was wrong with this Proverbs 31 Woman?* I wondered. *Does God have a sense of humor? Was He playing a joke on me? Why would He give me a ministry nobody else wanted or even liked? Why would He give me a ministry Anna Hayford hates?* There had to be more to this than I knew.

Of course, she was kidding, but I would have never expected to hear that from her. Anna Hayford was the epitome of the Proverbs 31 Woman and a virtuous wife to her husband, Pastor Jack and a wonderful mother to their four children. She has an excellent spirit in every way. I know she's an accomplished cook. In fact, she's written numerous cookbooks. She once told me she sewed all the curtains in her home and had her own garden. Anna fears the Lord and has loved and served Him faithfully all her life. The Lord has used her to lead many people into the kingdom of God. **"She shall rejoice in time to come, A woman who fears the Lord, she shall be praised,"** Proverbs 31:30 says. That's Anna! Isn't that a perfect picture of a godly woman? Of course it is! So what's to hate?

What's to Hate?

Anna's facetious remark about the Proverbs 31 Woman was nothing more than a throwaway line, long forgotten by her. But I didn't forget it. God used that statement as a thought provoking catalyst to stir up my curiosity in order to study, research, and dig for answers. Answers as to why this "woman" was universally disliked and I presumed; very misunderstood. Why did women everywhere love to hate her?

As I said, Anna Hayford is the perfect Proverbs 31 Woman. The fact is, most of us were trying to live up to her example. So what's to hate? The truth is Anna's amused dislike of the Proverbs 31 Woman is not unlike the rest of us Christian women. Most of us view the lofty, seemingly unobtainable character, work ethic—including the myriad of tasks, duties, and accomplishments of this virtuous wife—as ridiculous. Women resent being forced to live up to the impossible standards mentioned in these verses. Over the years, I've heard it said that this woman is only a representation or personification of all women rolled into one. As you read on, you will see that is partially true.

How Can This Be One Woman?

Is it even humanly possible for one woman to do and be all that is written of this Proverbs 31 woman? Think about it. She is not only a virtuous wife and mother, which are full-time jobs in and of themselves, she was well traveled, a successful investor and an entrepreneur (a venture capitalist!), an early riser, a seamstress, a philanthropist, a designer, a good cook, and a merchant. She also had time to be charitable, caring, and kind. And don't forget blessed and much, much more!

What always bothered me about these Proverbs 31 verses is "she" is defined as a "wife" right up front. She has to be a wife. A virtuous wife! There were many stringent qualifications to adhere to. At what age does she qualify to be a P. 31 W.? Does she ever get too old? What happens if she becomes a widow? Is she immediately kicked out of the Virtuous Wife Club? Maybe to her dismay she never married. And, she also MUST be a mother. What if she is a wife but, was barren and never able to become a mother? What if her only child were to die, or her husband? Is she automatically disqualified? Is she asked to leave the Proverbs 31 group? What if she married a scoundrel and her husband ran around on her, humiliated her, and then divorced her for another? Perhaps a younger woman? What happens then? After all of that, is she then kicked out of this small, elitist group? How shameful! Isn't this chapter much more about character than life's uncontrollable circumstances and injustices?

That doesn't sound like the God I know, who shows no partiality and is no respecter of persons or gender. Galatians 3:28 says, "There is neither Jew nor Greek, slave nor free, there is neither male nor female, for we are all One in Christ." As believers, we are one in Christ, like His church, His body, and the beloved bride of Christ.

As I became more familiar with Proverbs 31, I was thoroughly convinced there was more to these verses than appeared on the surface. There was deeper meaning. I was determined to uncover what was really being said here. I began to believe there were probably layers of untold revelation and understanding yet to be uncovered.

So it was at this time in 1996 that I began to purchase a plethora of choice books, including Hebrew dictionaries, lexicons, commentaries, and concordances galore. I began to pray, study, research, and dig for answers. God lit a raging fire in me, and I was determined to discover His hidden truth about this woman to redeem her perfect past and yet, bad reputation. The beauty and benefit of this detailed study is this, I learned how to study the entire Bible like this. I couldn't get enough! My appetite was insatiable for the Word of God.

I immediately began to discover some of the hidden truths necessary to 'redeeming' this woman. Little did I know these twenty-two simple verses were speaking prophetically of a woman who was indeed the "redeemed."

Proverbs 25:2 says, **"It is the glory of the Lord to conceal a matter, But the glory of Kings is to search out a matter."**

Finally, the Revelation

I believe this Proverbs 31 Woman to be greatly misunderstood because this entire chapter has been completely misunderstood. After many years of studying the original Hebrew words that made up the text, I've come to understand it as a non-gender specific, spiritual metaphor for God's entire church, which includes every believer in the body of Christ but personified as a virtuous wife through Christ's virtue abiding in her. Spiritually and prophetically speaking, it is God's beloved bride in Christ. She is submitted and committed to her Bridegroom King, Jesus Christ, just as in marriage. They are one through covenant, much like a husband and wife.

Who Is The Virtuous Wife?

I began by studying the mysterious and unknown King Lemuel, whom the Bible says penned the Proverbs 31 verses. No one seems to know who he is. I found out in the *Strong's Concordance* that Lemuel was a nickname for King Solomon. In Hebrew, "Lemuel" means "belonging to God." The Talmud says Solomon was called by six names: Solomon, Jedidiah, Koheleth, Son of Jakeh, Agur, and Lemuel.

1 Kings states that King Solomon was the wisest of all men. I believe this king, filled with the spirit of wisdom roughly 950 years before Christ, saw a prophetic picture of a day in the Lord on the horizon, where there would be a faithful bride and a virtuous wife to and for God. "She" would be in direct contrast to the unfaithful and idolatrous nation of Israel, whom God called His chosen, His people, and He called Himself their Husband. Israel was accused of being unfaithful and called a harlot, God says in Jeremiah 3:1. God goes on to say in Jeremiah 3:14, **"I am married to you."** In Ezekiel 16:32, God calls Jerusalem "an adulterous wife." As God betrothed Himself in covenant to beloved Israel like a husband, He quickly discovered they were not faithful, or virtuous, to Him but instead, an adulterous people. Once called the "virgin daughter" by the prophets, Israel did not and would not remain pure and holy unto the Lord and was headed for destruction. Idolatry turned virgin Israel into a harlot. God was heartbroken over their disobedience, stiff-neck and continued stubbornness, which led to their destruction.

But God had a man (the Son of Man) and a plan, and King Solomon clearly saw this virtuous wife and faithful bride, who was to come.

Proverbs 31:10 asks, **"Who can find a virtuous wife?"** The tone suggests one is difficult to find. I say, a virtuous wife is hard to find because she is hidden with Christ in God. (see Colossians 3:3)

The Virtuous Wife—An Army?

"Who can find a virtuous wife?" Don't you find it interesting that the very first verse making up the Proverbs 31 chapter, opens up with a question? Until now, even God couldn't find a virtuous wife. The Hebrew word for "virtuous" is *cha-yil* and is #2428 in the *Strong's Concordance* and is defined as an army. It also means a force, might, power, strength, virtue, valor, and war. Isn't it curious the definition is made up almost entirely of military terms? It certainly does not sound like the description of a wife. When was the last time you described a woman as an army? Explain that to me, please.

This 'virtuous wife' is defined in the next line: "Her price is far above rubies." Her *price?* In ancient Israel, this was called the "bride price" given by the bridegroom's father for his son's new wife. But I believe King Solomon was prophetically seeing and referencing Jesus and His bride, and most assuredly, her price was far above rubies. It cost the life and the ruby red blood of the Father's only Son, Jesus Christ, shed for His church, His beloved Bride, to redeem and buy her back in order to reconcile us to the Father once and for all. Paul says, speaking to the Corinthian believers in 1 Corinthians 6:20, **"For you were bought at a price."** Jesus paid the ultimate price to purchase His beloved bride. He paid with His life.

Warrior Princess Juliana Parker

I believe the virtuous wife chapter of Proverbs 31 was a prophetic picture of God's faithful and beloved bride in Christ, including every man, woman, and child. That's why I purposely chose to picture the youthful and innocent Juliana Parker on the title page for this chapter to represent God's warrior princess. As a young believer, she's already a 'virtuous wife' having entered into a holy covenant with God through Jesus Christ and is filled with His Spirit and therefore, filled with His divine virtue. At eleven years old, she's prepared, ready to serve, and ready to meet her Maker. As His bride, we are an army of one, made up of many. Let's not forget two of the multiple names of God in the Bible are the Commander of the Army and the Lord of Hosts.

Proverbs 31:11 says, **"The heart of her husband safely trusts her; so he will have no lack of gain."**

"For your maker is your husband, the Lord of Hosts is His name; and your redeemer is the Holy one of Israel; He is called the God of the whole Universe" (Isaiah 54:5).

The Father of the Bride

The moment you heard about Jesus and believed in your heart and confessed with your mouth and then made Him your Savior and the Lord of your life by saying, "I do, I do believe," you got "married." You entered into a holy, sanctified union, much like marriage, when you entered into a holy covenant with God. Since His creation of mankind, He has always wanted to be in communion with us. His longing to be one with us was established and accomplished through the crucifixion, burial, and resurrection of His only Son. In becoming one with His Son, we were reconciled to God, our heavenly Father. Now through the indwelling of His Holy Spirit within us, we are finally one. Only His virtue in us, through and by His Spirit, can empower us to be His virtuous wife. We are deplete of virtue outside God's power and virtue dwelling in us.

Verse 11 says, **"The heart of her husband safely trusts her."** Jesus is not only our husband but also the hidden man of our heart. He safely trusts us because His Holy Spirit lives in us and leads and guides us into all truth, all the time. And we are called and equipped to lead others into that truth. In so doing, "He will have no lack of gain,' or growth in the kingdom of God, as we are used to increase, advance, and enforce His kingdom. That's the picture of the Warrior Princess in action. Hallelujah! That's our job. I can't speak for you, but I do not want to be an unprofitable servant to my Lord.

Daughters or Brides?

So are we His daughters or brides, you ask? When I asked the Father that same question a many years ago, this is how He explained it to me. We are all created by God to be His children and a member of His family. The Father only has one Son. As soon as we receive His Son into our life as Lord and Savior, and

He becomes our betrothed Bridegroom King, we simultaneously became God's daughters. We married into the family! In Israel, the betrothal covenant is as honored and legally binding as marriage itself. When we receive, or "marry," His Son, God becomes our Father. So technically, we are both the daughters of God and the Bride of Christ, even though the Father and Son are one.

Jesus Christ — in Us

Virtually every verse is a picture of Jesus Christ living His life in and through us as His virtuous wife. For example, Proverbs 31:13 says, **"She willingly works with her hands."** Who else do we know who willingly worked with His hands? Jesus. That word "worked" actually means "sacrifice" in the *Strong's Concordance.* Jesus willingly sacrificed with His hands in giving up His life for the world.

Verse 14 reads, **"She brings her food from afar." Jesus did that, too. In fact, He said, "I am the Bread of life. This is the bread which comes down from Heaven, that one may eat of it and never die"** (John 6:48, 50). He was and is the Bread of Life sent from heaven. Now that's "from afar."

Verse 15 reads, **"She also rises while it was yet night."** John 20:1 tells us, **"Now on the first day of the week Mary Magdalene went to the tomb early while it was still dark and saw that the stone had been taken away from the tomb."** It says of Jesus, it was **"still dark," and He had already risen! We, as believers, have risen with Christ. Colossians 2:12 says, [we were] "buried with Him in baptism, in which you also were risen with Him through faith."** She, His virtuous wife, has also risen with Christ.

Verse 19 reads, **"She stretches out her hands to the distaff and her hand holds the spindle."** The most commonly used word for distaff was "staff," and the most commonly used word for spindle was "rod," during the time this was written. She has a rod and a staff in her hands. This is clearly a woman who is a shepherdess created in the image of the Good Shepherd.

Verse 20 reads, **"She extends her hands to the poor and the needy."** Jesus certainly did that. He extended His hands on the cross as He died to pay the price for our sins. We are all poor and needy. We are all sinners who need a Savior. He wants us to extend our hands and share the bread sent from heaven with those who have never tasted the Bread of Life.

Seven different times in the Proverbs 31 text it says she uses her hands to share and to give. There is much symbolism being spoken of here, because the number 7 in the Bible always speaks of spiritual perfection and completion. That's a picture of God's virtuous wife—complete in Him. The Lord would say to you, "Yes, the kingdom of God is at _hand,_ and it begins with yours and mine." Just like this Proverbs 31 virtuous wife did.

The Woman at the Well

The NT is written in Greek. The Greek word *hora* means "hour" or "day." 2 Peter 3:9 says, **"That with the Lord one day is as a thousand years and a thousand years is as a day."** Based on that verse, it's safe to say we are living in the sixth hour or day. It's been two days or two thousand years since Adam to Abraham, and two days or two thousand years from Abraham to Jesus. And it has been two days or two thousand years since Jesus until now, for a total of six thousand years. It was the sixth hour of the day that Jesus met the woman at the well in John 4:6. It was after she met and spoke with Jesus and believed Him to be the long-awaited Messiah that she went into the city of Samaria and told them about Jesus. Many believed in Him, also.

The sixth hour being spoken of in the Bible is prophetic regarding how mightily women will be used in this sixth day or sixth hour before His return. Much like John the Baptist, we will prepare the hearts and minds of those who don't know Him yet, so they too, will come to know Him as their personal Lord and Savior.

The woman at the well was the first evangelist! God calls every one of us who has drunk from that well, the well of salvation, to share the good news of the living water that only Jesus offers. He wants us to dig wells of salvation in the hearts and minds of those who know Him not. Jesus said in John 7:38, **"He who believes in Me, as the scripture has said, out of his heart shall flow rivers of living water."** Jesus, the living water within us, will be used to cleanse, bless, and refresh others in His holy name as we lead them to Him. Freely you have received; now freely give.

We live in an hour, sisters, we've never seen anything like before in the history of humankind. God has used women and will continue to use us to spread the gospel as never before. Don't forget that Jesus chose and trusted women at the garden tomb to be the first to know, see, speak with and then to share with the other disciples the good news of the Lord's resurrection. He had risen, just as He had promised (see John 20:1–18). As it began, so shall it end with Him using women.

As we, each a Proverbs 31 Woman, await the return of our Bridegroom to retrieve us, Christ in me urges you to be ready and prepared for that coming hour. Let your vessel be filled and ready. As His beloved bride, He wants to touch, heal, fill, and use all of us. It will take every one of us to fulfill the Proverbs 31 Scriptures. That is precisely why she is so focused and busy. In Proverbs 31:27, we are told not to eat of the bread of idleness. Not any one woman can accomplish all that is spoken of in those well-known and lofty verses. It takes us all doing our part.

The great preacher Charles Spurgeon once said about the bride of Christ, "That God has made rich provision for all of her needs, paid all of her debts, has allowed her to share in all of His wealth and walks in His name with full authority to advance the Kingdom of God." That's the virtuous wife God has always wanted.

God's Virtuous Wife Is You!

Are you surprised at what you have just learned? Are you convinced that you are indeed the virtuous wife King Solomon spoke of almost three thousand years ago? I hope I've explained well, my journey into God's knowledge, wisdom, and understanding regarding this virtuous woman.

Now that you know this well-hidden truth about the spiritual identity of the Proverbs 31 Woman, you'll no longer need to hate her. After all, "she" is you, and *you* are His virtuous wife, and together, we are one in Him, as His beloved bride. What a great mystery this is!

All faithful believers, young and old, single and married, and male and female are the betrothed bride of Christ and His virtuous wife. He has empowered and anointed all of us to teach, preach, and reach out to share the life changing truth of the gospel of Jesus Christ with others in need. Extend your heart and hands to the poor and needy. That includes every person who has not received Jesus as Lord and Savior. As Jesus said, "The Kingdom of God is *at hand,*" and I say it begins with yours and mine. Our heart and hands giving God's love away!

Proverbs 31:29 says. **"Many daughters** (*daughters* is the Hebrew word *ben*, which means sons or builders of the family name) **have done well** [virtuously] **but you excel them all."** Why does this 'daughter' excel them all? Because she is God's daughter, the beloved bride of His Son, she fears the Lord and is busy building His Kingdom. Verse 11 says, [because of her] **"He will have no lack of gain."**

Doting Daughters

As God's Proverbs 31 'virtuous wife,' in Christ, let's agree together and individually to be the Warrior Princess and the 'doting daughters' our Heavenly Father is depending on us to be. We can't do it alone, but must all do our part to;

Spread His Word,
Shine His Light,
Share the gospel of Jesus Christ.
Let's get started sisters, we've got no time to waste!

Unless noted otherwise, all scriptural references were taken from the New King James Version of the Thomas Nelson New Spirit Filled Life Bible.

This chapter was written by Shauna Mayer. Her contact information for ministry is;

Shauna Mayer Ministries
P.O. Box 55876
Sherman Oaks, CA 91413
818 8551404 0ffice
818 3241456 secondary
Email: Shauna@ShaunaMayerMinistries.org website: ShaunaMayerMinistries.org